Sedona Relocation Guide

A Helpful Guide for Those Thinking of Relocating to Sedona, Arizona

William Bohan

Nancy Williams

Non-liability Statement

The information contained in this work was correct at the time of first publication. But changes occur for various reasons and the reader is cautioned to determine if the information is still accurate. All opinions contained herein are those of the authors and do not necessarily represent the opinions of others contained in this work.

ISBN-13: 978-1478179917
ISBN-10: 1478179910

Front cover photo: view looking north at Uptown Sedona
Back cover photo: the authors having lunch along Oak Creek

Table of Contents

Acknowledgments

We'd like to acknowledge the many people who contributed to this work. They include: Roberta Avery, John Avery, Michele Braun, Rene Braun, Ruth Butler, David Butler, Jody Cibak, Starla Collins, Leslie Hunt, Steve Hunt, Peg Likens, Tom Likens, Traci Lowe, Greg Luckey, Helen Mueller, Becky Solon, Tom Solon, Lorna Thompson, Darryl Thompson, Marilyn Weaver, Charlie Weaver and Amy Whitehill.

Introduction

Sedona, Arizona. Those words have a certain magic ring to those of us who have chosen to live here. If you've been to Sedona, you know exactly what we're talking about. If you haven't yet experienced Sedona, you will understand as soon as you first arrive.

Like so many others who now live in Sedona, we came as tourists. William caught a very intense case of "Red Rock Fever" as soon as we rounded 'that' corner on State Route (SR) 179. We'll explain that in the chapter, "Sedona Stories." Though Sedona strongly beckoned us, deciding to move to Sedona was a carefully considered decision for us. It was a process over several years of visiting and gathering information on the community as well as getting a 'feel' for the Sedona environment. The main reason for this book is to provide others with information that they may need in considering a move to Sedona. Its purpose is to aid in the decision making process and answer the very important question: Should I move to Sedona?

Inside you'll find a short history of Sedona. You'll discover what services are available for residents and understand Sedona's cosmopolitan, rural nature as a small town with millions of visitors annually. We've included references and information on where to obtain the latest information about services, programs and volunteer opportunities as these can change over time. Finally, you'll read the personal stories of people who decided to move to Sedona.

Yes, Sedona is a very special place. We hope that by reading this guide, it will help you decide if Sedona is your special place. If you have comments or suggestions for us regarding this guide, please email us at: bill@billbohan.com.

Good luck!

William and Nancy
Sedona, Arizona

Chapter 1

What Makes Sedona so Special

"Sedona" actually consists of the City of Sedona and the Village of Oak Creek (VOC), which is approximately 7 miles south of the City. Both share a "Sedona" mailing address, although with differing zip codes. The City is about 19 square miles in size and straddles two Arizona counties, Coconino and Yavapai. The population as of the 2010 Census was approximately 11,300.[1] Elevation of the City is approximately 4,500 feet.

The VOC is approximately 4.6 square miles in size, all of which is in Yavapai County. The population in 2010 was approximately 6,350.[2] Elevation in the VOC is approximately 4,350 feet. Additionally, surrounding developments outside of the City and the VOC raise the population in the area by approximately 1,000.

Sedona is located near many attractions. The Grand Canyon is a 2 hour drive. Las Vegas is a short 4 ½ hour drive. San Diego is 7 hours away. This central location makes Sedona a perfect base for traveling to these and other destinations.

It's estimated that somewhere between two and four million visitors come to Sedona each year. So, ask yourself, "Why do these visitors from all over the world come to this small town in Arizona? And why is it that most of the people who live here are from somewhere else? What makes Sedona so special?" We'll try to explain that next....

If you ask a first-time visitor to Sedona why they came, they'll likely say that they heard about Sedona from a friend. Once you visit Sedona, it seems, you can't help but rave to your friends about Sedona's beauty, art, culture and outdoor activities. Other first-time visitors will say they read an article in a newspaper or magazine about Sedona.

---

1   Source: http://www.usa.com/86336-az.htm
2   Source: http://www.usa.com/86351-az.htm

More than half of all visitors to Sedona have heard about Sedona's vortexes.[3] Vortex energy is thought by some to be a concentration of the life force of the earth. This force has been described at various locations around Sedona as being positive, negative, masculine, feminine, upflow or downflow, electrical, magnetic, electromagnetic or examples of sub-atomic particles that are a part of "string theory." So many theories from so many interesting sources is just one of the intriguing and inspirational aspects of Sedona. Each person who visits chooses their own truth about vortex energy. It is a personal journey.

If you ask a local person what makes Sedona so special, you'll receive many answers. Some like the numerous activities in the arts and culture. Some like the access to the Coconino National Forest for hiking and bicycling. Some are fascinated with the geology of the region. Others like the mild climate and proximity to other attractions. Still others will say that they feel like they have come "home." Many say that it is the people... the residents who welcomed them as though they were family. You'll read about what makes Sedona so special to these people in the chapter entitled, "Sedona Stories." The thing about Sedona is that you live in Sedona because you want to, not because you have to.

There is no denying the beauty of the red rocks as a major reason why Sedona is special. Visitors and locals alike are mesmerized by them. As the sun moves across the sky, the red rocks change in their appearance so that each time you look, it appears that you are viewing a scene you haven't seen before.

There is something intangible about Sedona that makes it special. When visitors arrive in Sedona, many of them immediately feel a peace within themselves. All of a sudden a feeling of finally "coming home" affects many. They just know they have to be in Sedona. Some would say that it is the vortex energy of Sedona that is affecting them. Others say it is the majestic beauty that overwhelms the senses. We're not sure what it is exactly – we just know it exists; affects many people and is called "Red Rock Fever" locally.

When you first arrive in Sedona, you may experience this "Red Rock Fever." It has happened to many of the current residents. It is characterized as an overwhelming desire to be in Sedona. If you catch it, and many do, you will either be compelled to move to Sedona or return

---

3 Recreation Guide to Your National Forest, Red Rock Country – Coconino National Forest – Sedona, Arizona, page 11

again and again. In the section titled, "Sedona Stories," we offer you an interesting glimpse into other residents' journeys to Red Rock Country. You'll read how "Red Rock Fever" affected some of the people who now reside in Sedona and how they came to live here.

Relocating to Sedona is not strictly a matter of demographics, weather, shopping or educational opportunities alone. Yes, they all play a role in the decision to move to Sedona, but relocating to Sedona is an emotional choice, not necessarily a logical choice.

Sign located on SR 179 near Sedona city limits

Chapter 2

Sedona Then and Now

Sedona's geological history has interested geologists for many years. The creation of what is now Sedona's red rocks is a fascinating story best told by the experts who have studied these majestic mountains. To give you a glimpse of what geologists have discovered about Sedona's landscape, we offer a brief summary.

Some 350 million years ago, Sedona and the surrounding area was the floor of a salt water sea. It took 30 million years until rock sediments began to collect beneath that sea. Over the next 65 million years, the region where Sedona is located changed again and again. During those years, these red rock mountains were shaped by tropical seas, river floodplains, desert sands and coastal winds to finally produce the amazing red rocks we enjoy today. [4]

One question that visitors always ask is: What makes the red rocks red? In Wayne Ranney's _Sedona Through Time_, he answers this question exceptionally well. He explains, "Simply put, there is a thin coating of red, iron oxide mineral on the outside of each individual sand grain. The amount of iron giving the color in Sedona's red rocks is only about one half of one percent by weight of the rock! An individual sand grain from within the red rocks would barely look pink in color. There is not a lot of iron that makes these deep red colors. The sandstones originated as deposits in the windblown dune fields or river floodplain environments. The source area for these environments were the Ancestral Rocky Mountains, an area of granite mountains."[5] If you would like a very detailed picture of how this region was formed, we would recommend you read Mr. Ranney's book.

No one knows when the first human actually saw the red rocks, but it probably occurred about 11,500 years ago with the mammoth hunters. Later, the Sinagua Indians, descendants of the Hohokam, fished and

---

4   Wayne Ranney, Sedona Through Time (Zia Interpretive Services, 2001) pp.5 - 41
5   Ibid, page 10

farmed nearby and harvested wild desert plants for medicinal and practical uses. Their ancient homes, occupied between 550 and 1400 A.D., still dot the area today. Honanki and Palatki Heritage Sites; Montezuma Castle and Montezuma Well National Monuments; Tuzigoot National Monument and V-Bar-V Heritage Site offer the public a glimpse into pre-Sedona life.

In 1876, under the Homestead Act, one of the earliest white settlers in the Upper Oak Creek area, J.J. Thompson, took squatter's rights to a parcel of land across from today's Indian Gardens Trading Post. He found a water spring, and built a log cabin. As the years passed, more canyon settlers followed who raised horses and cattle and dug irrigation ditches for orchards. Apples and pears raised near Oak Creek were sold at markets in Jerome, Cottonwood, Phoenix and Los Angeles. During the ensuing decades, the trails and cow paths in the canyon became dirt roads.

In 1879, the Abraham James family moved to the area known then as Camp Garden (formerly known as Upper Oak Creek), which would later be called Sedona. The James family named Bell Rock and Steamboat Rock, among others.

In 1899, Theodore (Carl) and Sedona Schnebly moved to Camp Garden (Upper Oak Creek). In 1902, the couple purchased an 80-acre site near the present day Los Abrigados Resort and Tlaquepaque Arts and Crafts Village upon which Carl constructed a large house with two stone fireplaces. There the Schneblys grew fruit and produce; operated a general store and ran a hotel in their home.

Carl soon recognized the need for regular mail service, so he filed an application for the establishment of a post office. He proposed the names, "Oak Creek Crossing" and "Schnebly Station," but the Postmaster General in Washington rejected the names because they were too long to fit on a cancellation stamp. He then submitted the name of his wife, Sedona, as suggested by his brother, Elsworth. On June 26, 1902, postal officials approved the name "Sedona" and the post office was launched.

Throughout the Twentieth Century, the Sedona area continued to grow, slowly at first. Electricity finally came to Sedona in 1939. After WWII, Sedona experienced its most dynamic growth. During the 1940's and 1950's, Hollywood "discovered" Sedona, even though there were only about 500 residents. Sedona was featured in nearly 40 Western films produced during that period.[6]

By 1960, major home subdivision developments were underway as a result of the discovery of an aquifer for water supply under Sedona. Land exchanges with the U.S. Forest Service consolidated dispersed parcels of land. Between 1945 and 1960, some sixteen land exchanges in the Sedona area were completed. The beauty of Sedona was calling to the affluent middle class retirees who found the mild climate, abundance of outdoor activities and solitude perfect for retirement. A dynamic real estate industry developed which helped to sell Sedona to admiring visitors.

The City of Sedona was incorporated in January, 1988. There are approximately 11,300 residents in the City of Sedona with between two and four million visitors arriving yearly to marvel at the red rocks. About 7 miles south of the City is the VOC, home to about 6,350 residents. Also known as Big Park, the VOC serves as the gateway to Sedona as travelers driving north on SR 179 to Sedona pass through the VOC where they encounter the named rock formations of Bell Rock and Courthouse Butte.

Driving north on State Route 179 in the VOC. Bell Rock on the left; Courthouse Butte on the right

---

6   For more Sedona history, contact the Sedona Heritage Museum, (928) 282-7038

Chapter 3

Sedona Real Estate Considerations

There are many real estate options in Sedona such as single family homes or condominiums for sale or rent. Also, there are vacant lots for sale if your Sedona dream is to build your own home, though vacant land is becoming a premium in the Sedona area. Many people who relocate to Sedona find that purchasing a home then renovating it to suit their life style and needs is advantageous. Some of the more established homes have the best views in Sedona. A strategy that some future residents choose is to purchase a property then rent it to others as they work toward their retirement and subsequent move to Sedona. These properties could be located in the City of Sedona (zip code 86336), the VOC (zip code 86351), in an unincorporated portion of either Coconino or Yavapai Counties, or in one of several nearby communities. This chapter will discuss some of the considerations and alternatives to help with your decision.

Working with a Real Estate Professional

If you are interested in purchasing property, one of the first steps you should take is to make contact with a professional real estate agent/broker. The Sedona real estate market is constantly changing. Properties come and go off the market, sometimes very quickly. Establishing a relationship with a real estate professional is essential. Before contacting a real estate professional, it is expedient to have a definite idea of the type of property that you are searching for, the price range within your budget and the desired location. Once you begin the process of the hunt, stay with that real estate professional. Sedona is a small town so many, if not all, of the realtors know one another. If you look at properties on your own and you meet another real estate professional, be sure to inform them that you are working with another agent/broker. That way, you are assured of the best outcome possible because the two professionals can coordinate their efforts to give you the best service.

The California Comparison

In general, Sedona real estate is expensive. That said, people from high cost real estate markets like California find prices to be a bargain. People from locations where real estate prices are less than California find Sedona real estate to be costly. Because Sedona is surrounded by the Coconino National Forest, developed real estate is somewhat limited. This fact results in a premium applied to developed Sedona real estate.

The Red Rock View Factor

People move to Sedona to enjoy the red rocks. On the first visit to Sedona, visitors stay in hotels or resorts that feature magnificent views of the red rocks. When people move to Sedona, they want to have similar views in their home. Subsequently, this helps to create a high demand for  homes that have unobstructed views of the red rocks. Hence, as the red rock view gets better, you'll find that the price of the property increases proportionally.

The Location Factor

Certain areas around Sedona seem to command higher prices than others. Because there is a certain mystique to living in Uptown Sedona and the Chapel area,[7] properties in these areas are typically priced higher than those in the VOC or West Sedona, all other things being equal. Property prices are generally higher in West Sedona than those in the VOC. All of these areas are considered to be Sedona but have differing zip codes as we mentioned earlier.

Properties located in surrounding communities like Cornville and Cottonwood are typically priced less than Sedona, sometimes about half of Sedona's price, all other things being equal.

---

7   The Chapel area refers to homes built near the Chapel of the Holy Cross, approximately 3 miles south of the intersection of SR 89A and SR 179.

Map of Zip Code 86336[8]

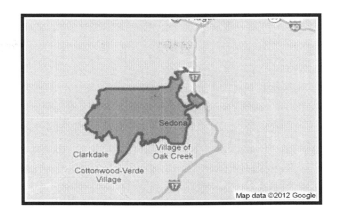

Map of Zip Code 86351[9]

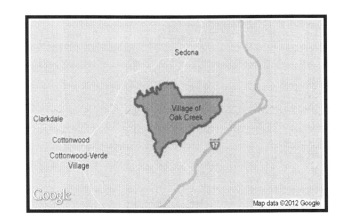

Home Sales Data

Sales of homes in and around Sedona have recently suffered the same fate as home sales across the nation. Because people considering relocating to Sedona could not easily sell their home where they currently live, they have been unable to buy a home in Sedona. This has produced a slowing of the real estate market in Sedona over the past few years (2006 – 2011) resulting in some excellent buying opportunities for those able to purchase.

---

8   Map from http://www.city-data.com/zips/86336
9   Map from http://www.city-data.com/zips/86351

13

Home Sales in Zip Code 86336 (City of Sedona)

The following graph shows home sales data for zip code 86336. It shows that both the number of home sales and the median sales price have fallen from 2006 to 2011. In 2006, there were approximately 700 sales with a median sales price of about $450,000. In 2011, there were approximately 400 sales (a 43% reduction) at a median sales price of about $280,000 (a 38% reduction). The year 2008 was particularly bad for the number of sales, although the median sales price did not drop proportionally with home sales. It appears that the real estate market has stabilized somewhat with the number of sales and the median price remaining relatively constant through the year 2011.[10]

10 Map and data from http://www.city-data.com/zips/86336

Home Sales in Zip Code 86351 (VOC)

A similar trend is evident in zip code 86351. While there are fewer number of sales in the VOC (because fewer homes are available as compared to the City of Sedona), the trend toward fewer sales is also present. In 2006, there were approximately **425** sales at a median sales price of $500,000. However in 2011, there were approximately **220** sales (a reduction of **48%**) at a median sales price of $295,000 (a reduction of **41%**). It appears that the real estate market is also stabilizing in zip code 86351.[11]

It is difficult to directly compare the median sales prices between zip codes 86336 and 86351 because the former includes several areas that were built up many years ago and include modular, smaller homes. Construction in zip code 86351 tends to be newer with fewer modular type homes.

Buying a Rental Property

The Sedona area has an active rental market. There are approximately **2,375** renter-occupied properties in zip code 86336 and **1,320** renter-

11 Map and data from http://www.city-data.com/zips/86351

15

occupied properties in zip code 86351.[12] Thus, one alternative method to enter the Sedona real estate market is to purchase a rental property. In some cases, the rental income is enough to pay the mortgage, repairs, taxes and other expenses associated with the rental property. This situation can vary widely so be sure to check with your accountant.

There are two types of rental properties in Sedona, short-term vacation and long-term rental property.

Vacation rental properties are rented for short-terms, a minimum of 30 days (City and County Ordinances) to several months. The property should include furniture and amenities consistent with the rent collected. Management, advertising and cleaning expenses will normally be high. And the unit(s) probably won't be rented all the time.

Long-term rental property is usually non-furnished with lease terms of six months to one year. Occupancy rates are ordinarily higher than with vacation rentals, but the monthly rent will be less. Because there is less tenant turnover with long-term rental property, the management fees and cleaning expenses will usually be less.

The typical expenses associated with either type of property include:
- management expenses – 10% of the gross rent
- property taxes – 1-2% of the property value
- insurance – 0.25% of the property value
- mortgage expense
- homeowner association fees
- repairs – 0.25% of the property value
- miscellaneous expenses

If you are considering purchasing a property to enter the rental market, your real estate professional can help you with a financial analysis of the property so that you understand what the cash flow and profit or loss will be. You also should consult with a professional property management company for an evaluation of any positive or negative aspects of a particular property as part of your buying process even if you plan to manage the property yourself.

---

12 City-data.com, Ibid

Future Sedona Development

Sedona is surrounded by the Coconino National Forest. The only way more land can be developed in Sedona is if a land trade is accomplished. In past years, if a developer had land desirable to the U.S. Forest Service somewhere in the U.S. and the U.S. Forest Service had land in the Coconino Forest around Sedona it wished to trade, then, after a lengthy administrative process, the two parties swapped those parcels of land. Currently, land trades are highly restricted under Amendment 12 of the Coconino Forest Plan for the Sedona area. Efforts are underway to designate the area around Sedona as a "National Scenic Area," which would have the effect of prohibiting land trades altogether.

Buying a Vacant Lot

The number of vacant lots is much smaller than in years past, but vacant lots are still available. As with buying a home, the price of vacant lots is determined by location, size and red rock views. Lot prices in Sedona can range from $100,000 to over $1 million. City sewer system hookup is not available for all vacant lots in the City or in the VOC. Some vacant lots require an aerobic septic system, which can be expensive to install. Other lots can have a "normal" septic system installed. Natural gas is not universally available in the City or the VOC, which requires that heating systems use electricity or propane. Also, in some areas, there is no cable access for computer or television reception. Be sure to work with your real estate professional to determine availability of utilities for any vacant lot you are considering.

Building Contractors

There are many excellent building contractors in Sedona who can construct your "dream home" on your vacant lot. A list of builders is available from the Sedona Chamber of Commerce.[13]

---

13 For more information, go to: http://www.sedonachamber.comand and click the link to contractors/home builders.

17

Chapter 4

Sedona Weather

Sedona enjoys a moderate year-round climate with about 330 days of sunshine each year. Because Sedona sits at an elevation several thousand feet above Phoenix, temperatures in Sedona are approximately 10 to 20 degrees lower. Winter in Sedona can be cool, with nighttime temperatures averaging about 32°F. However, temperatures have been known to be as low as 10°F. It is not unusual to see snow in Sedona several times between December and March of each year. But the snow melts quickly because the daytime temperatures can rise to 50°F – 60°F with most days full of sunshine. Temperatures and weather conditions vary considerably within the Sedona area because of elevation changes from one locality to another. The residents do enjoy this aspect of local weather. One local anecdote is that it can be sunny in the VOC while a rain or snow storm is raging in the West Sedona area. Elevation differences within the City and the VOC will affect what plants can be grown in different locations.

Summertime temperatures can rise to 100°F or more. This usually happens only a few days each summer. At night, temperatures cool down so that there is relief from the hot daytime temperatures. Many people open their windows after dark and, with the breeze and cooler temperatures, the need for running air conditioning units is minimized.

Summertime outdoor activities are usually performed early in the day. Hikers, for example, may start at 6:00 am (note that the sun rises shortly after 5:00 am in the summer months) and be finished by 10:00 am.

Humidity in Sedona is usually very low, except during the monsoon season. In July, August and early September, the monsoon rains are evident. At times there are flash flood warnings because several inches of rain can accumulate in a very short time.

Tornadoes are extremely rare for the Sedona area. Thunderstorms during the monsoon season and high winds any time of year are common. The danger of wildfires is a potential threat throughout the year.

Below is a table showing monthly average Sedona temperatures, monthly precipitation and sunrise/sunset times.[14]

	Sedona Weather				
	Temperatures (F)				
Month	Average Low	Average High	Precipitation (Inches)	Sunrise	Sunset (15th of Each Month)
January	33	58	2.07	7:34 AM	5:39 PM
February	35	61	2.10	7:13 AM	6:10 PM
March	38	66	2.23	6:37 AM	6:35 PM
April	44	74	1.09	5:55 AM	7:00 PM
May	52	84	0.58	5:23 AM	7:24 PM
June	60	93	0.27	5:13 AM	7:43 PM
July	66	96	1.53	5:25 AM	7:41 PM
August	65	94	2.13	5:48 AM	7:15 PM
September	60	88	2.01	6:10 AM	6:33 PM
October	50	78	1.52	6:33 AM	5:52 PM
November	39	66	1.33	7:02 AM	5:22 PM
December	32	57	1.71	7:28 AM	5:17 PM
Average	48	76	1.55		

All in all, the moderate climate of Sedona permits outdoor activities such as golf, hiking and tennis to be enjoyed year round. Some adjustment to starting times may be necessary in the warm summer months but overall, you can enjoy the outdoors throughout the year.

Snow in Sedona as seen from Schnebly Hill Road

---

14 Sources: http://weather.com for temperatures and precipitation data:
    http://aa.usno.navy.mil for sunrise/sunset data

Chapter 5

Sedona Arts, Culture and Events

Sedona hosts many arts, culture and entertainment events. The art scene is dominated by the Sedona Arts Center and the many galleries here. The area from the Hillside Shopping Center to the Tlaquepaque Arts and Crafts Center is commonly known as "Gallery Row." There is a more concentrated number of fine galleries in this area. But you'll find galleries throughout the Sedona area. Cultural events include plays and concerts at the Sedona Red Rock High School Performing Arts Center.

Throughout the year, you'll find a wide variety of ongoing community events. For example, on the first Friday of each month, members of the Sedona Gallery Association sponsor a First Friday Tour where artists and special exhibits are featured at various galleries that create a friendly atmosphere by offering refreshments. The Sedona Trolley is sometimes used to shuttle locals and visitors between the galleries for free.

Chamber Music Sedona sponsors many events throughout the year including live simulcasts of the Metropolitan Opera.[15]

Additionally, each month finds a number of other events occurring. These events may change each year but a typical year's events are shown below:[16]

February

The Sedona Marathon attracts runners, joggers and walkers from all over the world to enjoy the scenic 26-mile course. There is also a 5K, 10K and half marathon run.

---

15 For more information, go to: http://www.chambermusicsedona.org/
16 For the latest Sedona event calender, go to the Sedona Chamber of Commerce website: http://visitsedona.com.

The Sedona International Film Festival attracts independent film makers from around the world to showcase their latest offerings. There are workshops in various film making disciplines presented by top names in the field. Celebrities are honored during this week-long event.

Sedona Bridal Fair is a venue where local businesses demonstrate their services such as photography, wedding cakes and location selection to the expanding market for weddings held in Sedona.

March

St. Patrick's Day Parade and festival is fun for everyone. The morning parade is followed by a festival in Uptown Sedona with live music and entertainment, food booths and a beer garden.

April

Verde Valley Birding and Nature Festival increases the awareness of the importance of habitat on all life in the Verde Valley. There are educational workshops, recreational activities and area food vendors. The event is held at Dead Horse State Park in Cottonwood.

Bike Ride Sedona is a two-day event which raises money for the Multiple Sclerosis Society.

May

The ZGI Shorts Film Festival is two days of independent short films; learning about career opportunities and film making equipment.

The Sedona Bluegrass Festival is several days that showcase emerging and established bluegrass artists. Concerts are often held in a beautiful setting beside Oak Creek.

June

The Sedona PhotoFest features symposiums given by top American photographers; an exhibition and sale of photographs submitted and evening talks on how to improve photographs.

Sedona Taste is held along Oak Creek and is a celebration of fine food and drink prepared by some of the Verde Valley's finest restaurants.

July

4th of July Laser Light Show held at Posse Grounds Park is a presentation of lasers choreographed to music by local musicians.

Day of the Cowboy is celebrated in Uptown Sedona with performances by gunslingers, ropers and western music entertainers. Western art is displayed.

August

Red Rocks Music Festival is a week-long affair with chamber music, orchestral performances and workshops.

Sedona Hummingbird Festival includes demonstrations, banding and informative presentations.

September

Midnight Madness Street Festival includes free music and entertainment, children's activities and sidewalk sales centered around Uptown Sedona.

Fiesta Del Tlaquepaque is held at Tlaquepaque Arts and Crafts Village and consists of food, entertainment and music.

Sedona Airport Family Fun Day is held at the Sedona Airport and features displays of aircraft and classic vehicles , children activities, food and entertainment.

Sedona Winefest is held at the Sedona Airport where local wineries offer their wines for tasting and gourmet food is available. There is live entertainment and displays of art from the Sedona Arts Center.

October

Sedona Arts Festival is held at Sedona Red Rock High School where fine art and crafts are exhibited. Cuisine from Sedona restaurants is available.

Sedona Plein Air Festival brings many of the country's top plein air artists to Sedona.

November

Red Rock Fantasy consists of twenty-five displays of holiday-themed subjects using nearly one million lights.

Holiday Tree Lighting is a ceremony held annually in Uptown Sedona where the lights on a large decorated Christmas tree are turned on. Santa and holiday music are featured.

December

The Festival of Lights at Tlaquepaque Arts and Crafts Village includes thousands of glowing luminaries, dancers and entertainers.

Sculpture located in Uptown Sedona

Chapter 6

Taxes in Sedona

Sedona visitors, part-time residents and full-time residents are all affected by taxes. The Arizona tax structure relies heavily on the sales tax and is one of the highest in the U.S. The taxes you could be subjected to are discussed next.

Sales Taxes

In Arizona, the tax on retail sales is called a Transaction Privilege Tax, which is commonly known as a sales tax. Arizona also levies a Use Tax, which is equal to the sales tax. It applies to out-of-state purchases or internet purchases where no equivalent Arizona sales tax has been paid. In addition to the state sales tax, all fifteen Arizona Counties levy a sales tax. And many cities, including the City of Sedona, add an additional sales tax to retail purchases.

In general, the combined sales tax rate (the total of the state sales tax plus county and local sales tax) throughout Arizona is more than 9%. Arizona ranks as the second highest combined sales tax rate in the U.S., behind only Tennessee.[17]

Not everything you buy is subject to sales tax. For example, drugs prescribed by a physician or dentist and food for home consumption is not taxed but alcoholic beverages and restaurant meals are subject to sales tax. Services are not taxed such as haircuts or beauty parlor services. If you purchase a used motor vehicle from an individual, sales tax is not charged. However, if you purchase a used vehicle from an automobile dealer, sales tax will be charged.

---

17 Source www.taxfoundation.org

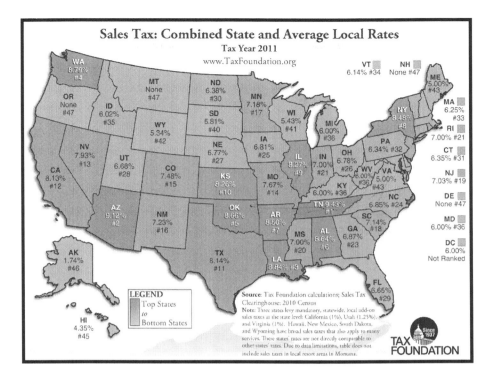

Sales Tax: Combined State and Average Local Rates
Tax Year 2011
www.TaxFoundation.org

Source: Tax Foundation calculations; Sales Tax Clearinghouse; 2010 Census

Note: Three states levy mandatory, statewide, local add-on sales taxes at the state level: California (1%), Utah (1.25%), and Virginia (1%). Hawaii, New Mexico, South Dakota, and Wyoming have broad sales taxes that also apply to many services. These states' rates are not directly comparable to other states' rates. Due to data limitations, table does not include sales taxes in local resort areas in Montana.

In the Sedona area, the sales tax rate can be more than 10% and varies depending on where you purchase the merchandise. Sales tax rates are:

- 10.725% in the City of Sedona, Coconino County

- 10.375% in the City of Sedona, Yavapai County

- 7.35% in the VOC

Property Taxes

There is no state property tax, nor is there a City of Sedona property tax, but there is a county property tax. The property tax is administered by county assessors and collected by the county treasurer. Property taxes include assessments for the county, the Sedona Unified School District, Yavapai or Coconino Community College, Sedona Fire District, libraries, flood control districts and other miscellaneous jurisdictions. Typically, the property tax due on a property is approximately 1% of the market value.

Single homeowners 65 and older who earn less than $3,750 and married couples who earn less than $5,500 are eligible for a tax credit of up to $502. Persons at least 65 years old who have resided in their primary residence for at least two years and have a total income not more than four times the Social Security Supplemental Security Income (SSI) benefit rate may apply to the assessor by September 1st to have the valuation of the primary residence and up to 10 acres of adjoining undeveloped land frozen at the full cash value when the application is filed.

Personal Property Taxes

Arizona also taxes personal property, which is defined as all types of property except real estate. Taxable personal property includes property used for commercial, industrial and agricultural purposes. As a resident without a commercial business, personal property taxes do not apply.

Motor Vehicle Taxes

In lieu of a personal property tax on automobiles, the state imposes an annual motor vehicle license tax (VLT). The VLT is based on an assessed value of 60% of the manufacturer's base retail price reduced by 16.25% for each year since the vehicle was first registered in Arizona.

For example, for a new vehicle that costs $25,000, the first year assessed value would be $15,000 and the VLT would be $420.00. The second year the assessed value would be $12,562.50 and the VLT would be $363.06.

There is a $4.00 title fee; an $8.00 registration fee; plus an air quality research fee of $1.50. There may also be a weight fee and commercial registration fee, if the vehicle is registered as commercial. For a mobile home the title fee is $7.00 per section or unit.[18]

---

18 For more information, call (800) 251-5866.

State Income Tax

Arizona has a graduated state income tax with rates between 2.59% and 4.54% based on on Adjusted Gross Income (AGI).

AZ AGI - Single	AZ AGI - Married	Marginal Tax Rate
$0 to $9,999	$0 to $9,999	2.59%
$10,000 to $24,999	$10,000 to $49,999	2.88%
$25,000 to $49,999	$50,000 to $99,999	3.36%
$50,000 to $149,999	$100,000 to $299,999	4.24%
More then $150,000	More then $300,000	4.54%

Arizona's top marginal income tax rate of 4.54% is the fourth lowest in the U.S. Most deductions allowed on Schedule A for federal income tax are allowed by Arizona. In addition, all medical expenses may be deducted. Other subtractions from income include an exemption for individuals age 65 or over, interest on U.S. Savings Bonds and Social Security income included in your federal return.[19]

Estate, Inheritance and Gift Taxes

There is no estate, inheritance or gift tax.

---

19 For more information, go to: http://www.azdor.gov/Individual.aspx

Chapter 7

Medical Facilities

The availability of healthcare providers is a consideration when contemplating any relocation. In Sedona, there are personal physicians, dentists, eye care providers, etc. who accept new patients. Be sure to check with your health care insurer for medical services covered by your insurance and if the Sedona medical provider is accepting new patients.

Regarding medical facilities, Sedona has excellent medical facilities nearby which consist of the Verde Valley Medical Center (VVMC) in Cottonwood, VVMC Sedona Campus and the Flagstaff Medical Center (FMC) in Flagstaff.

Verde Valley Medical Center[20]

VVMC in Cottonwood is a full-service, 99-bed, non-profit hospital serving North Central Arizona. More than 800 professional and support staff are employed at VVMC. The medical staff is comprised of nearly 100 physicians representing twenty-five medical specialties. VVMC is licensed by the State of Arizona; certified by Medicare and accredited by DNV.[21] It is a member of Northern Arizona Healthcare that serves patients through FMC, Heart & Vascular Center of Northern Arizona (HVCNA), Cancer Centers of Northern Arizona Healthcare, Guardian Air and Northern Arizona Homecare and Hospice.

---

20 For more information, call (928) 634-2251 or (928) 639-6086 website: VerdeValleyMedicalCenter.com

21 DNV Healthcare is an accreditor of US hospitals integrating ISO 9001 quality compliance with the Medicare Conditions of Participation.

VVMC Sedona Campus[22]

VVMC Sedona Campus provides high quality healthcare to Sedona residents and visitors. It consists of two primary care offices staffed with board-certified internal medicine providers and a pediatric physician. The 43-acre Sedona Campus on SR 89A in West Sedona consists of:

* 24-Hour Emergency Services[23]

* The Cancer Centers of Northern Arizona Healthcare providing radiation and medical oncology services with board-certified oncologists who utilize the most current technologies and programs including the Breast Cancer Resource Center and Nurse Navigator Program, brachytherapy, intensity-modulated radiation, image-guided radiation therapy, support groups and more. The Center is affiliated with the University of Arizona Cancer Center (UACC).[24]

* HVCNA providing a comprehensive line of cardiology services including electrophysiology, diagnostic, traditional and minimally invasive surgical treatment options. It also provides a regionalized approach to the delivery of cardiovascular services, including diagnostic and intervention catheterization for cardiac/vascular disease and cardiothoracic (open heart) surgical procedures.

* EntireCare Rehab & Sports Medicine, with facilities also in the VOC, providing physical, occupational and hand therapy; comprehensive sports medicine therapy and speech/language therapy. Licensed therapists provide rehabilitation after injury or surgery, as well as treatment to decrease pain and increase range of motion for chronic degenerative conditions.

---

22 For more information, call (928) 204-3000 website: VerdeValleyMedicalCenter.com/SedonaCampus
23 For more information, call 24-Hour Emergency Number: (928) 204-4160 website: VerdeValleyMedicalCenter.com/OurServices/EmergencyServices
24 For more information, call (928) 204-4160 website: VerdeValleyMedicalCenter.com/OurServices/CancerCenterSedona

VVMC Specialty Programs in Cottonwood

The VVMC Specialty Programs consist of:

- Cardiovascular Services providing on-site angioplasty and stent placement. Intervention cardiologists are available 24/7 for diagnoses and treatment of emergency and non-emergency cardiac care. A cardiac rehabilitation program through monitored health and fitness sessions is also offered.

- The Orthopedic and Joint Replacement Program providing preoperative education, state-of-the-art surgical techniques and pain management strategies.

- EntireCare Rehab & Sports Medicine providing physical, occupational, hand and speech therapy.

- Level I Perinatal Center providing labor and delivery, obstetric, nursery and pediatric care.

- Senior Lifestyles providing assessment and treatment for seniors experiencing medical and psychiatric conditions. Consistent with a holistic treatment philosophy, the recovery process places equal emphasis on the healing of mind, body and spirit.

- Other services including a multi-service, certified clinical laboratory; 24-hour emergency department with on-site medical helicopter; surgical services; hemodialysis and a variety of other services.

Flagstaff Medical Center[25]

FMC is Northern Arizona's only regional referral center, caring for more than 85,000 patients each year. It provides comprehensive, state-of-the-art healthcare from diagnostic outpatient services to open heart surgery.

FMC services include:

- Level I Trauma Center providing care to critically injured patients.

- Advanced Cardiovascular Services providing advanced heart and vascular care consisting of a full range of cardiac care, open heart surgery and minimally invasive procedures.

- State-designated Cardiac Arrest Center providing comprehensive, technologically advanced care to patients experiencing sudden cardiac arrest.

- da Vinci Robotic Surgery used for minimally invasive weight loss and general surgery.

- Spine and Joint Surgery Center providing a unique surgical approach to those patients who require total joint replacement or spine surgery.

- Bariatric Surgical Weight Loss Center providing a comprehensive program, for not only weight loss surgery, but also patient education and support for morbidly obese patients choosing a surgical solution.

- The Cancer Centers of Northern Arizona providing a multi-disciplinary team designed to ensure the cancer patient's treatment is individualized, comprehensive and coordinated. The Center consists of radiation and medical oncologists, physicists, radiation therapists, certified oncology nurses, social workers and dietitians. The Breast Cancer Resource Center provides education, resources and support services for women undergoing treatment and their families. The Nurse Navigator Program provides guidance, emotional support and care management to those recently diagnosed with cancer and their families.

---

25 For more information call (928) 779-3366 website: Flagstaffmedicalcenter.com

Sedona Urgent Care[26]

The privately-owned Sedona Urgent Care facility provides care for minor emergencies, illness or injury on a walk-in basis. It provides services for:

- Minor Emergencies
- ADOT Physicals
- Sports Physicals
- Boy/Girl Scout Physicals
- Seasonal Flu Shots
- Seasonal Allergy Injections
- Employment Drug Screens
- Workers' Compensation Injuries
- On-site Digital X-Ray and Limited Lab Services
- Limited Pharmacy for Patient Convenience

---

26 Sedona Urgent Care is located at 2530 West SR 89A, Sedona, Arizona 86336. Telephone (928) 204-4813. For more information, go to: http://www.sedonaurgentcare.com/index.html.

Chapter 8

Education

Public Schools

The Sedona-Oak Creek Joint Unified School District[27] consists of:

- Sedona Red Rock High School

- West Sedona Elementary School

- Big Park Elementary School

Private Schools

There are a number of private elementary and college preparatory schools in the area. The Sedona Chamber of Commerce has an online link to Community & Professional Services, Schools/Tutoring.[28]

Colleges and Universities

There are three institutions of higher learning nearby. They are:

- Yavapai College offering classes in Sedona and surrounding communities

- Coconino Community College offering classes in Flagstaff and beyond

- Northern Arizona University, located a short 45-minute drive away in Flagstaff

---

27 For more information, go to: http://www.sedona.k12.az.us/
28 For the latest information on private schools in the Sedona area, go to:
     http://www.sedonachamber.com

Cultural/Unique Schools and Libraries

- The Zaki Gordon Institute for Independent Filmmaking offers a one-year curriculum in all aspects of film making. Credits are transferable to Northern Arizona University.[29]

- Yavapai College has a unique program called the Osher Lifelong Learning Institute (OLLI) of Sedona and Verde Valley. It was created to meet the needs of intellectually active adults. Classes are held in Sedona and there are no grades or tests. Members can either teach classes in areas of their expertise or attend classes for the joy of learning and enrichment of their lives.[30]

- Sedona has a privately-run public library, which opened in 1994, and is located at 3250 White Bear Road in West Sedona. A satellite library is located at Tequa Plaza, Suite C102, 7000 SR 179 in the VOC.[31]

- The Sedona Art Center offers classes in painting, pottery, sculpture, photography and more.[32]

Statue of Sedona Schnebly at Sedona Public Library

29 For more information, go to: www.zgi-yc.com.
30 For more information, go to: https://www.yc.edu/v4content/lifelong-learning/olli/default.htm
31 For more information, go to: http://www.sedonalibrary.org/
32 For more information, go to: http://www.sedonaartscenter.com/

Chapter 9

Shopping in Sedona

In the Sedona area the resident shopper must be resourceful, creative and patient. The shopping composition of this area is created by city and county zoning and building ordinances; expensive, scarce available land upon which to build commercial buildings; the millions of visitors who come to Sedona and an insufficient population to support large chain or big box stores. In addition, many of the residents moved here because of the scenic, small town nature of Sedona and want to preserve that aspect of the area.

We support shopping locally. But, if you are accustomed to driving a few blocks to do some "power shopping," you won't find that here. If large big box, chain, or department stores are your passion, then Sedona shopping will disappoint you and the shopping experience will be a huge adjustment. Because of the two to four million visitors who arrive in Sedona each year, the retail environment is one that is geared to the tourism industry. Restaurants, lodging establishments, souvenir stores, art galleries, tour operators and the like make up the majority of businesses in Sedona. On the other hand, Sedona is home to some very unique boutique shops that make the shopping experience very personal and friendly. Local residents get to know the shop owners which can lead to some very nice price reductions....not always but frequently.

To "power shop," many residents plan day trips down to Phoenix/Scottsdale (110 miles), Flagstaff (40 miles) or Prescott (45 miles). This mode of shopping has become fun and delightful for some of us. A girls' shopping day trip really lifts the spirits in so many ways.

If renovating or furnishing a home, there are local stores that offer what a homeowner might be searching for. There are several stores selling new furniture, some with a southwestern/Mexican influence. Sedona also has a number of consignment and thrift shops where gently used

35

furniture and other household items are available. However, for a wider selection of merchandise and prices, traveling to the Phoenix/Scottsdale, Flagstaff or Prescott areas is what many of the residents do. Often, the result is making purchases from merchants in all of these locations.

There is an outlet mall and several smaller malls located in the VOC but the majority of shopping is located in the City of Sedona, primarily in West Sedona.

There are three large grocery stores within the City (2) and the VOC (1). Each grocery store has a well-equipped pharmacy and there is a national brand pharmacy located in West Sedona. There currently is one natural food store and another under construction in West Sedona as of this writing. A large building supply company (for lumber, plumbing, electrical and other supplies) is located in West Sedona. There are two national brand hardware stores - one in the City and one in the VOC.

To purchase electronics, televisions, appliances etc. requires a trip to Cottonwood (20 miles), Flagstaff, Prescott, or Phoenix/Scottsdale. To shop at large "super centers," a trip to these cities is a must.

There are several excellent automotive service businesses and two tire stores in Sedona. But to purchase a new vehicle or have service performed at an authorized dealer, you must drive to Cottonwood, Camp Verde, Flagstaff or Prescott. Some Sedona residents drive to Phoenix/Scottsdale to purchase new vehicles.

There are a number of health clubs, hair salons, spas and massage facilities available. Many are world famous because they cater to celebrities and tourists from around the globe.

Finally, there is the convenience of online shopping. Often, many will shop online which affords the shopper worldwide access to merchandise.

Chapter 10

Places of Worship

There are many faiths represented in Sedona and many places to worship. They include but are not limited to:

Amitabha Stupa
P.O. Box 1142
Sedona, AZ 86339
www.amitabhastupa.org

Christ Center Wesleyan Church
580 Brewer Road
Sedona, AZ 86336
(928) 282-9767

Christ Lutheran Church
25 Chapel Road
Sedona, AZ 86336
(928) 282-1022
www.christsedonaelca.org

Church of Jesus Christ of LDS
160 Mormon Hill Road
Sedona, AZ 86336
(928) 282-3555

Church of the Golden Age
2645 Melody Lane
Sedona, AZ 86336
(928) 282-7900
www.churchofthegoldenage.com

Jehovah's Witnesses
110 Northview Drive
Sedona, AZ 86336
(928) 282-9290

Jewish Community of Sedona
100 Meadowlark Lane
Sedona, AZ
(928) 204-1286
www.jcsvv.org

The Master's Bible Church
175 Kallof Place
Sedona, AZ 86336
(928) 282-2155
www.masterbible.com

Sedona Church of Religious Science
333 Schnebly Hill Road
Sedona, AZ 86336
(928) 282-1446
www.sedonacrs.org

Sedona First Assembly of God
3132 White Bear Road
Sedona AZ 86336
(928) 282-7463

Church of the Red Rocks
54 Bowstring Drive
Sedona, AZ 86336
(928) 282-7963
www.churchoftheredrocks.com

Crestview Community Church
1090 W State Route 89A
Sedona, AZ 86336
(928) 282-7405

Sedona United Methodist Church
110 Indian Cliffs Road
Sedona, AZ 86336
(928) 282-1780
www.sedonaumc.org

St. Andrew's Episcopal Church
100 Arroyo Pinon Drive
Sedona, AZ 86336
(928) 282-4457
www.saint-andrews.org

St. John Vianney Catholic Church
180 St Vianney Lane
Sedona, AZ 86336
(928) 282-7545
www.sjvsedona.org

Chapel of the Holy Cross
780 Chapel Road
Sedona, AZ 86336

Sedona Seventh-Day Adventist
680 Sunset Drive
Sedona, AZ 86336
(928) 282-5121

Sedona Unitarian Universalist
Fellowship
P.O. Box 1670
Sedona, AZ 86339
(928) 282-5061
www.sedonauu.org

St. Luke's Episcopal Church
2690 State Route 179
Sedona, AZ 86336
(928) 282-7366
www.episcopalnet.org

Unity Church of Sedona
65 Deer Trail Drive
Sedona, AZ 86336
(928) 282-7181
www.unitysedona.org

Wayside Chapel Community Church
401 N State Route 89A
Sedona, AZ 86336
(928) 282-4262
www.waysidechapelsedona.com

NOTE: For the Chapel of the Holy
Cross, all masses are held at St. John
Vianney Catholic Church

Chapter 11

Clubs, Organizations and Support Groups

Sedona has many clubs, organizations and support groups. Here is a list of many with contact information:

National Clubs

The Rotary Club of Sedona

Contact:
http://www.sedonarotary.org

Sedona Red Rocks Rotary

Contact:
http://sedonaredrocksrotary.org/

Sedona Oak Creek Lions Club

Contact:
(928) 300-7141

Sedona Elks Lodge

Contact:
Sedona Elks Lodge 2291
110 Airport Road
Sedona, AZ 86336-5824
http://www.sedonaelks.org

Local Clubs

Sedona Car Club

Organized in 1982, the purpose of the club is to promote, preserve and maintain vehicles of special interest, but ownership of a "classic" vehicle is not required. The club meets once each month at the Sedona Public Library. The club sponsors driving tours, picnics, garage tours and dinners.

Contact:
email: info@sedonacarclub.com
http://www.sedonacarclub.com/index.html

Barbershop Singers of Sedona

The purpose of the club is to promote barbershop singing. The group offers quartet or chorus performances for any occasion. Meetings are held weekly.

Contact:
Barbershop Singers of Sedona
245 Concord Drive
Sedona, AZ 86336
(928) 282-2124

Sedona Area Garden Club

The purpose of the club is to advance gardening, promote civic beautification and conservation of natural resources. Activities include various garden projects at the Sedona Public Library and Sedona Arts Center. Food baskets are distributed at Christmas. The group meets once per month in a member's home. Membership is by invitation only.

Contact:
(928) 284-4759

Sedona Gem and Mineral Club

Monthly meetings are held at the Sedona Public Library with guest speakers, raffles and displays for local "rockhounds." Other club activities include monthly field trips to search for many different rocks, fossils and minerals. A rock and mineral show is held every October with a wide selection of vendors and materials.

Contact:
Sedona Gem and Mineral Club
P.O. Box 3284
Sedona, AZ 86340
email: webmaster@sedonagemandmineral.org
http://www.sedonagemandmineral.org/

Sedona Westerners

The largest hiking club in Sedona, the Westerners offer hikes into the red rocks and beyond for all levels of hikers. Hikes are arranged 5 days each week except in the summer months. The Westerners club was organized in 1961 and provides a means for hikers to socialize and learn about the native plants and peoples in the area. The members establish and maintain hiking trails and hiking signs in conjunction with the U.S. Forest Service.

Contact:
email: trailboss@sedonawesterners.org
http://www.sedonawesterners.org/index.shtml

Organizations

Yavapai Big Brothers Big Sisters

Yavapai Big Brothers Big Sisters enhances the lives of children through quality mentoring relationships. This private, non-profit organization, uses screened volunteers to act as friends, mentors and role models to school-aged children who are predominately from single-parent homes. These relationships are supported by a professional staff.

Contact:
Yavapai Big Brothers Big sisters
830 South Main Street, Suite 1-H
Cottonwood, AZ 86326
(928) 634-9789

The Hummingbird Society

The Society is a non-profit charitable organization, founded in 1996 and incorporated in Delaware. Its office is currently headquartered in Sedona. It was founded with the goals of teaching about hummingbirds and working to prevent their extinction. Meetings are at noon on the third Thursday each month.

Contact:
http://www.hummingbirdsociety.org
(800) 529-3699

Keep Sedona Beautiful

Keep Sedona Beautiful informs the community of environmental issues; contributes to a litter-free environment (litter lifters); and encourages the planting of native trees and shrubbery, etc. Its mission is: *"...acting through the stewardship of its members and volunteers, is committed to protect and sustain the unique scenic beauty and natural environment of the Greater Sedona Area."*

Contact:
Keep Sedona Beautiful, Inc.
Pushmataha Center
360 Brewer Road
Sedona, AZ 86336
http://www.keepsedonabeautiful.org/
(928) 282-4938

Support Groups

The following is a list of support groups in the Sedona area. For the latest information including meeting place, date and time, on any of these groups, consult the *Red Rock News*, Community Calendar.[33]

- Al-Anon
- Alcoholics Anonymous
- Alzheimer's Support Groups
- Bereavement Support
- Cancer and Caregiver Support Group
- Chronic Illness and Pain Support Group
- Debtors Anonymous
- Diabetes Support Group
- Fibromyalgia, Arthritis and Related Diseases Support Group
- Gamblers Anonymous
- Grandparents Raising Grandchildren Support Group
- Grief Support Group
- HIV-AIDS Support Group
- Kinship Kare of Northern Arizona
- Lamplighters
- Living with Loss
- National Alliance on Mental Illness
- Narcotics Anonymous
- Obsessive Compulsive Disorders
- Ostomy Support Group
- Overeaters Anonymous
- Parents, Families & Friends of Lesbian and Gays
- Parkinson's Disease Support Group
- Pet Bereavement Support Group
- Pregnancy and Postpartum Adjustment
- RI Discovery
- Sedona Sunrise Family Caregiver Alzheimer's Support Group
- Verde Valley Santuary Outreach
- Women's Cancer Support Group: Happy Huggers

---

33 This list from page 10A, May 30, 2012 Edition, Red Rock News

Chapter 12

Volunteer Opportunities

There are many opportunities to volunteer in Sedona. For example, you can deliver meals to shut-ins, help visitors find the perfect hiking trail, help at a hospital or show abandoned animals some kindness. Some of these volunteer opportunities are:

Sedona Public Library

Volunteers at the library assist patrons with checking out library materials and simple tasks such as printing, accessing email and saving files on flash drives. Other tasks involve pulling materials from library shelves; checking items in, then placing them on the library's hold shelf or in bins; issuing computer passes to library visitors and explaining how to log on to public computers.

Contact:
Sedona Public Library
(928) 282-7714, ext. 43

Verde Valley Caregivers

Volunteers provide a number of services for seniors in the Verde Valley including shopping for shut-ins; driving "neighbors" to doctor appointments and perhaps taking notes; installing "Guardian Angels" (personal alert systems) and scheduling Verde Valley Caregivers volunteers for their assignments. Hours are flexible and training is provided.

Contact:
Verde Valley Caregivers
(928) 204-1238

Sedona Heritage Museum

If you'd like to learn about the history of Sedona and volunteer in a historic building, the Sedona Heritage Museum may be the place for you. Volunteers interview long-time residents to capture their stories of early Sedona; organize displays of historic materials; make presentations to grade school classes, etc.

Contact:
Sedona Heritage Museum
(928) 282-7038

Sedona Humane Society

The Sedona Humane Society provides shelter for homeless and abandoned pets in the Sedona area. Volunteers help with special projects like posting flyers; work at the PetSmart Feline Adoption Center in West Sedona; greet visitors at the front desk or walk animals at the facility.

Contact:
Sedona Humane Society
(928) 282-4679

Volunteer Park Ranger

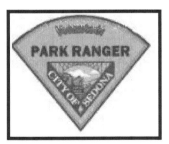

Volunteer Park Rangers provide periodic City of Sedona park patrols checking buildings and assisting park users. They also assist at City of Sedona Parks and Recreation Department sponsored events and occasionally perform light trail and maintenance work. Rangers provide information to visitors in Uptown Sedona and help at community events. They are provided a uniform, but must be willing to learn new skills and commit 2-6 hours a week.

Contact:
City of Sedona Parks and Recreation
(928) 282-7098

45

Meals-On-Wheels Drivers

Meals are delivered Monday through Friday (except on holidays) to home-bound seniors who are 60 years or older. Volunteer drivers deliver meals between 11:00 am and 12:30 pm. The Meals-On-Wheels driver may be the only human contact that the home-bound senior has for that day.

Contact:
Sedona Community Center
(928) 282-2834

Sedona Chamber of Commerce

Volunteers at the Uptown Visitor Center help visitors by providing information on shopping, lodging, restaurants, tours and recreation in Sedona. It's a great way to learn about Sedona too. Training is provided.

Contact:
Director of the Visitor Center
(928) 282-7722

Friends of the Forest

This non-profit, non-political organization is not strictly a volunteer organization, but offers many opportunities to do so. Membership is open to all who are dedicated to maintaining, protecting and restoring the scenic beauty of our National Forest lands in the Sedona area for the enjoyment and use of present and future generations. "Friends" volunteer at the Red Rock Ranger Station Visitor Center providing information on recreation in the forest surrounding Sedona. They perform hiking trail maintenance and assist with cultural and water sampling projects.

Contact:
Friends of the Forest
P.O. Box 2391
Sedona, AZ 86339

46

Verde Valley Medical Center (VVMC)

More than three hundred volunteers perform a number of activities including: book/magazine cart; helping in the cancer center; performing clerical duties; helping in the gift shop and at the information desk and providing internal transportation. All it takes is a willingness to spend 4 hours per week. Volunteers are matched with an assignment that fits with their personality, skills and schedule. Volunteer opportunities are available throughout all departments in Cottonwood and at the Sedona campus.

Contact:
Verde Valley Medical Center via email at:
https://www.myhospitalwebsite.com/NAH/view/VerdeValley/
GetInvolved/VolunteerServices/VVMCContactUsVolunteerServices

Red Rock State Park

Each year in September, six 4-hour training sessions provide prospective volunteers with information about park philosophy and the local area. Topics include natural sciences, the school environmental education program, maintenance, archeology, geology and interpretive hikes/tours. After graduation, volunteers then work throughout the park promoting environmental studies; lead programs and activities; assist park staff with maintenance projects or assist at visitor services.

Contact:
Volunteer Coordinator
(928) 282-6907

Slide Rock State Park

Volunteer positions are varied at Slide Rock State Park. They include: visitor services (entry fee collection, gift shop support, etc.), maintenance services (general maintenance and small construction projects), interpretive services (presenting educational programs, interpretive hikes, etc.) and special projects (developing interpretive programs, gardening, etc.).

Contact: Assistant Park Manager
(928) 282-3034

Flute player in Boynton Canyon

Chapter 13

Sedona Job Opportunities

Most of the people who move to Sedona are retired. Job opportunities in Sedona and the surrounding areas are primarily in the service industry. There are few, if any, manufacturing facilities nearby. With the millions of visitors to Sedona each year and the number of retirees who live in Sedona, it's not surprising that there are many positions for housekeeping maids, dishwashers and other jobs in the service industry.

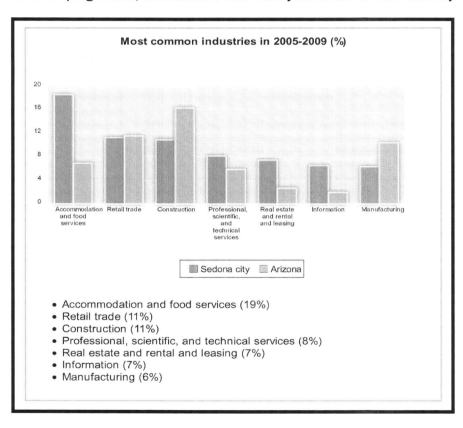

- Accommodation and food services (19%)
- Retail trade (11%)
- Construction (11%)
- Professional, scientific, and technical services (8%)
- Real estate and rental and leasing (7%)
- Information (7%)
- Manufacturing (6%)

As shown on the above chart, the most common jobs were accommodation (motel and hotel)/food service, followed by retail trade and construction for the years 2005 – 2009.[34]

The local newspaper, *The Red Rock News*, is published twice each week. In the Classified Section for a typical edition, the following "Help Wanted" ads appear:

Visitor Activity Positions		Lodging Positions	
ballooning crew	1	maids	4
traffic control	1	receptionists/bell staff	6
ATV washer	1	maintenance	7
Food/Restaurant Positions		marketing/accounting/security	4
chef part-time	1	**Retail/Sales Positions**	
dishwasher	3	time share sales	6
kitchen help	3	clothing/gift/jewelry/auto sales	5
servers	3	**Misc. Positions**	
coffee shop worker	1	auto mechanic/technician	2
cook for resort/B&B	4	truck drivers	5
supermarket clerks	4	certified teacher	1
Medical Positions		newspaper reporter/assembler	2
receptionists	2	landscape crew	1
caregivers	2	purchasing/shipping agent	1
nurses/therapist	2	cement plant workers	6

The Arizona Department of Economic Security maintains a web presence and a website that contains job information. You'll find information on job fairs, job search resources, unemployment benefits and employment programs.[35]

The closest Employment Services Office is in Cottonwood, Arizona at 1500 E. Cherry Street, Suite F, Cottonwood, AZ 86326. The telephone number is (928) 634-3337. There you can conduct a search of available jobs that potential employers have posted.

---

34 Source: http://www.city-data.com/city/Sedona-Arizona.htm
35 For more information, go to: https://www.azdes.gov/landing.aspx?id=1054.

The unemployment rate in Sedona is typical of the rate in the State of Arizona. While the rate has improved recently, it is still higher than the rate experienced in the 2000 to 2007 time period.[36]

Unemployment in March 2012:
Here: 8.7%
Arizona: 8.4%

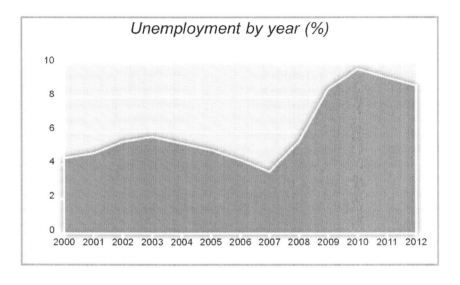

36 Source: http://www.city-data.com/city/Sedona-Arizona.htm

Chapter 14

Sedona is a Safe Place to Live

Sedona is a safe place to live. You will seldom encounter any dangerous animals or insects and the crime rate is very low. Problems in Sedona are primarily non-violent, i.e., traffic violations, burglaries or illegal drug use. *The Red Rock News*, the local paper, includes a 'Police Reports' column each week. It usually includes reports of DUI, suspended drivers' licenses and shoplifting reports. There are very few major crimes or murders committed in the Sedona area, although it can happen. Between 1999 and January 2012, two murders were reported in Sedona.

Probably the biggest concern to someone considering a move to the Sedona area are burglary reports because of the potential for a confrontation in the home or, if a home is left for long periods (as with a seasonal home), a break-in while away.

According to the Sedona Police Department, 38 burglaries were reported in 2011 and 50 burglaries were reported in 2010. The highest number of burglaries for the period 2000 to 2011 was 127 in 2003 and 88 in 2008.[37]

In the VOC, the Yavapai Sheriffs' Department reports that there were 8 burglaries in 2011, 26 burglaries in 2010 and 40 burglaries in 2008.

The burglaries seem to occur in daylight hours when the home owner is away. The burglar will usually knock on the door to determine if the home owner is at home first. Items taken are those that are easily concealed such as jewelry, cash and other small items.[38]

---

37 For the most current information for the City of Sedona, contact the Sedona Police Department at (928) 282-3100.
38 For the most current information for the VOC, go to: http://www.crimemapping.com/, Yavapai Sheriff link.

Another source for crime data, city-data.com supports the low crime rate in the Sedona area. For the years 2006 to 2010, city-data.com reports the following:

Crime in Sedona					
Type	2006	2007	2008	2009	2010
Murders	0	0	0	0	0
per 100,000	0.0	0.0	0.0	0.0	0.0
Rapes	3	3	2	6	6
per 100,000	25.8	26.1	17.3	51.0	53.4
Robberies	2	1	1	1	0
per 100,000	17.2	8.7	8.6	8.5	0.0
Assaults	18	5	19	20	11
per 100,000	154.5	43.5	164.1	170.1	97.9
Burglaries	43	84	88	65	50
per 100,000	369.1	731.5	759.9	552.8	444.8
Thefts	185	180	185	177	155
per 100,000	1588.1	1567.4	1597.6	1505.2	1379
Auto Thefts	13	11	4	4	5
per 100,000	111.6	95.8	34.5	34.0	44.5
Arson	0	3	4	2	1
per 100,000	0.0	26.1	34.5	17.0	8.9
Overall Crime Rate	125.8	124.8	137.2	145.3	123.5
U.S. Average	319.1				

The overall crime above rate uses a weighting factor so that more serious crimes add to the overall rate more than less serious crimes. Overall, crime in Sedona is about 2 ½ times less frequent than the average U.S. city.

Chapter 15

Recreation in Sedona

There are many ways to enjoy the outdoors in Sedona. They include: hiking, biking, horseback riding, camping, picnicking, outings at State Parks, golf and tennis. Here's a brief description of each:

Hiking[39]

Sedona has been called "the day hike capital of the world." With some 300 miles of hiking trails (trail heads are all close to or within Sedona), the ability to hike among the red rocks is an activity shared by thousands of people. Trails are available for all levels of hiking ability. There are trails that meander through forested canyons; lead to vortex sites (where many feel the earth's energy); follow a bubbling creek or feature panoramic red rock views. Hiking is enjoyable year-round (although summer hikes can be hot so starting very early in the morning is recommended). It is an inexpensive sport, requiring only a good pair of lug-soled shoes/boots (for traction); some type of pack to carry water; trail maps or an up-to-date hiking book (*Great Sedona Hikes Revised Second Edition* is an appropriate choice)[40] and protection from the sun. Optional equipment includes hiking poles, binoculars, a portable GPS unit with fresh batteries and a camera.

Biking[41]

Mountain biking is also very popular in Sedona. Cyclists come from all over the world to enjoy traversing the trails through the red rocks. Most of the hiking trails can also be used by cyclists, although there are some restrictions. There are several places to rent mountain bikes by the hour, day or longer in the Sedona area.

---

39 For more information go to http://greatsedonahikes.com
40 William Bohan and David Butler, Great Sedona Hikes Revised Second Edition (Create Space, January 2012)
41 See bike trails at: http://www.fs.usda.gov/activity/coconino/recreation/bicycling/

Horseback Riding

Equestrians also find that the hiking trails are well suited for riding. Several trail head parking areas have large pullouts for horse trailers. Again, many trails are suitable for horse and rider so they share those trails with hikers and bikers.

Camping

The U.S. Forest Service provides several locations for camping, some are along Oak Creek in Oak Creek Canyon. A description of nearby campgrounds in the Red Rock Ranger District follows:

Beaver Creek Campground

This 13-unit campground is sheltered by a stand of cottonwoods and Arizona sycamores clustered on the banks of Wet Beaver Creek. Tents, motor homes and trailers under 22' are permitted.

Cave Springs Campground

Cave Springs in scenic Oak Creek Canyon is one of the forest's most popular campgrounds. This 82-unit campground has 11 reservable sites. Tents, small motor homes and trailers under 36' are allowed.

Pine Flat Campground

Pine Flat Campground in scenic Oak Creek Canyon is also a popular campground. There are 56-unit sites, of which 18 are reservable. Tents, small motor homes and trailers under 30' are allowed.

Manzanita Campground

Located adjacent to Oak Creek, trailers and RVs are prohibited in this small, 18-unit campground. Tents and small sleep-in vehicles only are permitted. Drinking water, vault toilets (barrier free), fire rings and cooking grills are available.

Picnicking

The U.S. Forest Service provides several areas for picnicking, which require payment of various fees[42], including:

Midgley Bridge Observation Site

There are three picnic tables and a toilet available. Parking may be a problem due to congestion because the parking area is also the trail head for Wilson Canyon, Wilson Mountain, Huckaby and access to the Jim Thompson Trail.

Grasshopper Point Swim and Picnic Area

Nestled in the base of Oak Creek Canyon is a large cliff-side swimming hole known as Grasshopper Point. This day-use site is popular with swimmers and picnickers alike. The swimming hole is shaded and cool.

Crescent Moon Picnic Area

One of the most photographed scenes in the southwest is towering Cathedral Rock reflected in the waters of Oak Creek at Red Rock Crossing, which can be accessed from Crescent Moon Picnic Area. There are accessible picnic tables, cooking grills, vault toilets and a group ramada here.

Bootlegger Picnic Area

Located beside Oak Creek, you'll have a fishing hole with spectacular scenery, clear water swimming holes and excellent wildlife watching. There are picnic tables, vault toilets (barrier free), fire rings and cooking grills.

Encinoso Picnic Area

Encinoso is a 12-site picnic area that has picnic tables, cooking grills, drinking water and vault toilets (barrier free).

Banjo Bill Picnic Area

Banjo Bill is also an easily accessible picnic area with 12 picnic sites with tables and cooking grills. The area is adjacent to Oak Creek.

---

42 Some areas charge a separate entrance fee, others require that a Recreation Pass be displayed. For more information go to: http://www.redrockcountry.org/

Halfway Picnic Area

This picnic area is along Oak Creek with towering red rock cliffs and buttes. There are **8** picnic sites and vault toilets (barrier free).

Map of Campgrounds and Picnic Areas[43]

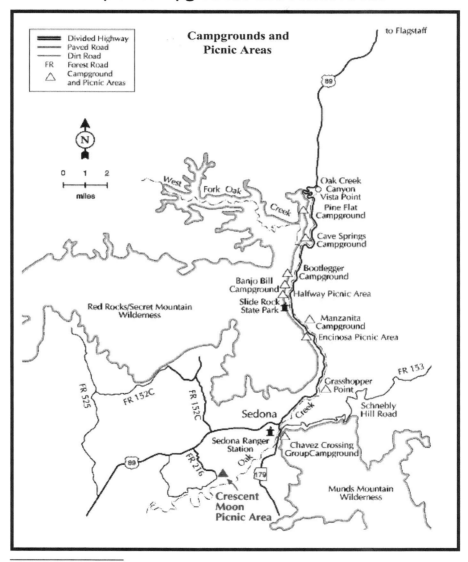

43 Map from http://www.fs.usda.gov

State Parks

There are two Arizona State Parks near Sedona, Red Rock State Park and Slide Rock State Park. Both have an entrance fee.

Red Rock State Park

Red Rock State Park is a 286-acre nature preserve and environmental education center with stunning scenery. It is open 7 days a week from 8 am – 5 pm. The Visitor Center is open 9 am – 5 pm daily. Trails throughout the park wind through manzanita and juniper that reach the banks of Oak Creek. Green meadows are framed by native vegetation and hills of red rock. The creek meanders through the park, creating a diverse riparian habitat abounding with plants and wildlife.

Red Rock State Park offers a variety of special programs for school groups and private groups. There are a number of daily and weekly park events (ask at the Visitor Center). Park facilities include a Visitor Center, classroom, theater, gift shop, picnic tables, ten developed trails, restrooms and a group area with ramada and facilities. The restrooms are handicapped accessible. Camping facilities are not available at this park.[44]

Slide Rock State Park

Originally the Pendley Homestead, it is a 43-acre historic apple farm located in Oak Creek Canyon. As one of the few homesteads left intact in the canyon today, Slide Rock State Park is a fine example of early agricultural development in central Arizona.

The park is named after the famous Slide Rock, a stretch of slippery creek bottom adjacent to the homestead. Visitors may slide down a slick natural water chute, wade in the cool water or sun along the creek. The swim area is located on National Forest land, which is jointly managed by Arizona State Parks and the U.S. Forest Service. The park becomes very crowded in the summer so arrive early or you'll wait to get in.[45]

---

44 For more information, go to: http://azstateparks.com/Parks/RERO/index.html

45 For more information, go to: http://azstateparks.com/parks/slro/index.html

Arizona State Parks Near Sedona[46]

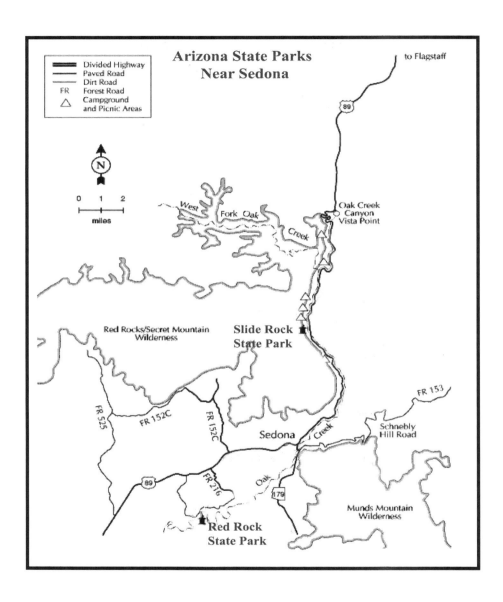

46 Map from http://www.fs.usda.gov

Golf

Oak Creek Country Club

The Oak Creek Country Club is a championship golf course nestled in the majestic Sedona red rocks with outstanding views. At this 5,600 to 6,800 yard par 72 golf course designed by Robert Trent Jones Sr. and Jr., the fairways are classic tree lined doglegs with fairway bunkers strategically placed in the landing areas and greens which are all slightly elevated and surrounded with large green-side bunkers.[47]

Sedona Golf Resort

This 6,646 yard, par 71 course is widely considered among the world's most unforgettable golf experiences. Winding around the famed red rocks of Sedona, each hole provides a unique adventure. If you could play golf in the Grand Canyon, this would be it. The championship Sedona golf course receives a continuous four-star rating from Golf Digest.[48]

Seven Canyons

The par 70 Seven Canyons golf course opened in 2002 and continues to receive rave reviews from the nation's foremost golf course critics and highly regarded golf publications. Designed by Tom Weiskopf, Seven Canyons is not long by modern standards, measuring 6,746 yards from the championship tees. There are small greens, narrow landing areas, classic-style bunkering, mature trees, natural water features and constant changes in elevation.[49]

Canyon Mesa Country Club

The 1,080 yard to 1,450 yard par 28 Canyon Mesa is a beautiful "Executive" course set amid a splendid background of Sedona's red rocks. Other than the shorter length, this nine-hole course has all the features of a championship course - great greens, some sand, water, and natural hazards. This is a great walking course, but electric carts are available for rent in the pro shop. Golf clubs to rent are also available.[50]

---

47 For more information, go to: http://www.oakcreekcountryclub.com/
48 For more information, go to: http://sedonagolfresort.com
49 For more information, go to: http://sevencanyons.com/golf.php
50 For more information, go to: http://www.canyonmesacountryclub.com

Verde Santa Fe Golf Course

This 5,430 yard to 6,325 yard par 71 course is located about 15 miles west of Sedona on the east side of Cottonwood. The course is framed by the vast Black Hills Range that extends from Camp Verde to Cottonwood. Here, Hogan's Wash and other natural arroyos come into play. Four lakes border the tenth and eighteenth holes.[51]

Pine Shadows Golf Course

The 2,003 yard to 2,223 yard par 33 Pine Shadows Golf Course is a nine-hole course located on the west side of Cottonwood, about 25 miles from Sedona. It features bent-grass greens, rye grass fairways and Kentucky bluegrass tee boxes. Located at the base of the Mingus Mountains, Pine Shadows Golf Course provides a fun golf experience for golfers of all skill levels. The course winds throughout the Mescal Gulch and the On the Greens senior gated community.[52]

Tennis

Many of the resorts in Sedona offer tennis to their guests and some permit non-guests to use their courts. Both the Oak Creek Country Club and Canyon Mesa Country Club have two courts each available for rent. In addition, tennis may be available at Sedona Tennis at the Red Rocks, formerly known as the Sedona Racquet Club, located in the Foothills South Subdivision. The club has fallen on some hard times and may not be open. It was founded in 1973 as a tennis facility. It was one of the largest clay court facilities in the western United States.[53]

Skiing

Winter snow skiing is available about 50 miles north in Flagstaff at Snowbowl. With 40 ski runs (15 beginner, 17 intermediate and 8 advanced), Snowbowl provides winter recreation between mid-December and mid-April (snowfall and weather permitting). Seniors 70 years of age and older ski for free.[54]

---

51 For more information, go to: http://www.verdesantafe.com
52 For more information, go to: http://www.pineshadowsgolfcourse.com
53 For more information, go to: http://srcs.us, or Sedona Chamber of Commerce.
54 For more information, go to: http://www.arizonasnowbowl.com

Chapter 16

Sedona Stories

In this chapter, we have gathered stories from people who dreamed of living among the red rocks of Sedona and how they achieved their dream.

Hal's Story

Hal, a California financial adviser, was told by one of his clients, "Hal, you really should go over to Sedona, Arizona and see the red rocks. They are beautiful."

Hal was interested in purchasing some rental property outside of California, so he began to plan a trip to check out Sedona and the Grand Canyon, then explore properties in Colorado.

In 1992, he flew to Phoenix and rented a car then drove north to Prescott, then to Jerome and finally, Sedona. On the way to Sedona, it started to rain heavily and by the time he arrived in Sedona, he was exhausted and very disappointed. Hal says, "You couldn't see more than ten feet in front of you, so no red rocks. The service at the restaurant where I stopped was lousy and the food cold. The hotel was all right but overpriced." He was not impressed with Sedona.

The next morning it was still raining in Sedona with visibility severely restricted. He drove the two hours up to the Grand Canyon where it was also raining, but had a wonderful time. After spending several days at the Grand Canyon, he was ready to drive east to Colorado. When he arrived in Flagstaff, the road east was closed because of flash flood warnings. At this point, because he couldn't continue on to Colorado to investigate rental property possibilities, he decided to return to Sedona on his way back to Phoenix.

Upon his arrival for the second time in Sedona, the weather had cleared and the sun shone. As Hal tells it, "I had never seen anything like it. Even though I had traveled throughout Europe and Asia, the sun on the red rocks was magnificent. I knew as soon as I saw Sedona's red rocks that I had to be here."

Hal had caught "Red Rock Fever," a condition that affects most of the people who decide to move here. He found a real estate agent who drove him around to the various areas in Sedona. When they drove in to the Chapel area (the subdivision located near and around the Chapel of the Holy Cross), he felt a very calming energy. The realtor showed him a vacant lot and Hal was hooked. He bought the vacant lot.

It took four years for Hal to wrap up his affairs in California and build his home on the lot near the Chapel. In 1996, he moved full-time to Sedona.

"I never bothered to check tax rates, availability of medical services, or any of those things I suppose you should check out before you retire to a place. But for me, there was no doubt in my mind that Sedona was the place I needed to be. I love the energy here and I wouldn't live anywhere else."

Chapel of the Holy Cross

William and Nancy's Story

William had never lived anywhere but Michigan. Nancy, a native of Texas, called Michigan home because she had lived there for many more years than she had in Texas. Nancy was sent as a representative of her company to a conference in Mesa, Arizona and William went along as the "spouse" - it was a great opportunity to take some much needed vacation time.

Before departing for Mesa, a good friend told them about an article she had recently read in the *Detroit News* about a place called Sedona. The article essentially said it was a very beautiful place, full of red rocks and "energy vortexes." William said, "What the heck! Why not check it out if the conference meetings end early?"

The conference lasted for five days. On Friday, the conference meetings ended earlier than scheduled at Noon. William and Nancy decided to check out the red rocks of Sedona to see what all the excitement was about. Nancy rented a car and made reservations at L'Auberge in Sedona. They began the 125-mile drive north toward Flagstaff around 1 pm.

The trip up the mountains through Black Canyon, Cordes Junction and the Verde Valley was scenic and interesting to two people more accustomed to the green grasses and trees of the Midwest. They enjoyed the colorful names of the washes like Bloody Basin and Dead Man's Wash. They joked about how could there possibly be red rocks in amongst all the barren desert soil, cactus and scrub. They reached Exit 298 where so many travelers before them had exited onto State Route 179 that leads into Sedona.

As they traveled along the scenic two lane road, William took out his video camera to record this historic event through the windshield as Nancy drove toward their destiny. Their anticipation was building as they went around each curve. About five minutes into this portion of the drive, they began to doubt that this was going to be as spectacular a sight as promised because the landscape was not changing from what they had already seen on their two-hour drive. Their impatience began to show and doubt increased. Then, at Mile Marker 304.4 as they came around the curve, there was the most breath taking sight that either of them had ever seen. Bell Rock, Courthouse Butte, Lee Mountain, Wild Horse Mesa, Castle Rock, etc. all revealed themselves. William was immediately overcome with the feeling that he had to live in Sedona. He had caught "Red Rock Fever."

William is a conservative engineer. He analyzes, plans, checks and double checks facts before he takes action. But within two hours of that first Sedona afternoon, they had met a real estate agent; been shown several vacant lots and had made purchase offers on two separate lots. The next day they were told that their offer on one of the vacant lots had been accepted. They were Sedona land owners! Being property owners in the Sedona area made them feel they had a vested interest in the community.

Though the desire to live in Sedona was compelling, they were both still working and about ten years from retirement. After some discussion, they agreed that resigning their positions to move to Sedona was impractical because they had too much invested in their respective corporations. So each December, they'd save vacation time and rent a house in Sedona for three to four weeks.

In 1990, they took another step toward their Sedona dream. They bought some investment properties, rental units in the VOC and Cottonwood. The rents were enough to pay all of the expenses and the mortgages on the units. Their real estate professional advised that appreciation on the rental properties would likely enable them to build a dream home when they were able to move to Sedona.

After they retired in 2001, they bought a condo in the VOC. They began to spend the winters in Sedona and return to Michigan from the spring through fall because of family ties there. But as time went by, they found they were spending more and more time in Sedona. The friends they made in Sedona became like family to them. The time away from Sedona and their friends seemed to become longer each year. They would count the time till they would return to Sedona rather than relish their time away in what used to be their home, Michigan. "Our social life in Sedona far exceeded that in Michigan and there were no longer family ties there," says William. In 2006, they sold their home in Michigan and constructed their dream home in the VOC.

Moving to Sedona after a lifetime in Michigan could have been a traumatic experience for William. But that wasn't the case. William knew he had to live in Sedona as soon as they came around that curve in 1989. "Nancy wasn't so sure at first, but now agrees that Sedona is the only place on earth for us to live. We love the ambiance of Sedona and the beauty of the red rocks. We like seeing snow for a short time in the winter (but we don't own a snow shovel – the snow is gone in a day or so). The summers can get warm, but the house cools down most evenings with the windows open so our air conditioning expense is minimal. Most of all, we love living in the Village because it's quiet and peaceful."

Beautiful Oak Creek

Rene and Michele's Story

Rene was born in Switzerland; studied to be a physician; then came to the U.S. for a medical internship where he met Michele, a nurse. After finally completing all necessary requirements, Rene and Michele moved to Minnesota and began a medical practice.

In 1978, a Native American friend told Rene, "You should visit Sedona. It's the most beautiful place." Later that year, Rene and Michele attended a medical conference in Flagstaff. At the conclusion of the conference, they rented a car and drove to Sedona, down Oak Creek Canyon on State Route 89A. As they drove into the small settlement that would become the City of Sedona, they were awe-struck by the red rocks. They looked at each other and said, "We have to live here."

After many years studying to be a doctor and starting a medical practice, money was tight. They decided that the $6,000 in their savings was the maximum they could afford for a lot in Sedona. The first several days of looking for a lot were spent in the VOC, which was just starting to develop. "All you could see were vacant lots and empty land. You had no idea what would be built there," says Michele.

They decided the City of Sedona was where they wanted to build their home. On one momentous day of searching, as Michele was pointing to the land up on a hill above the Sedona Airport, Rene asked, "Is anything for sale up there?" As it happened, a doctor was selling a vacant lot. After walking the lot, they knew they had to buy it. "The view is incredible," says Rene. Negotiations began. Rene and Michele eventually bought the vacant lot for $15,000. "We knew we'd have to make payments, since it was way over our budget, but the view from the lot was astonishing," says Michele. When they returned to Minnesota, friends asked, "How can you move to a place where you don't know anyone?" Michele replied, "Well, you just have to be adventuresome. We'll get to know people there. And besides, we know we have to live there [in Sedona]."

It took ten years for them to retire and build a home on that Sedona lot. After moving into their new home, Michele began to take classes in writing and painting at Yavapai College. It was a good way to meet new people. Some of the people she met in those classes remain friends some twenty-five years later. When they first lived in Sedona, they had an RV and used their Sedona home as a base for trips exploring the surrounding National Parks and attractions in Utah, California, Nevada and Colorado. They weren't concerned about the availability of medical services when they first moved to Sedona because they were relatively young and healthy. And now, there are good medical facilities.

"We knew immediately when we entered Sedona from Oak Creek Canyon in 1978 that Sedona was the place we wanted to live when we retired," says Michele. Their children live in the Midwest and wish Rene and Michele lived closer. However, when the children come to visit, they understand why Rene and Michele choose to live in Sedona.

Rene and Michele have lived in Sedona for nearly twenty-five years and stay active by hiking. They love the red rock mountain views of Sedona. Their advice to anyone considering moving to Sedona, "Don't wait any longer. Go for it. There aren't many buildable lots available anymore. And to meet people after you move here, reach out by taking classes or volunteering."

View of West Sedona and red rocks from Airport Scenic Overlook

Steve and Leslie's Story

Steve first visited Sedona in the 1980s, making a quick two-hour stop for lunch on the way up to the Grand Canyon from Phoenix. The next twenty years would find Steve and Leslie hard at work on the East Coast and in New York.

Steve worked as CFO for a group of Private Equity-backed companies and in 2003, those companies were in the process of being sold. Leslie, at this time, was a consultant for the American Red Cross and could arrange her schedule to have some time off. So in the summer of 2003, they decided to take a much-needed vacation and headed to Tucson, Arizona to spend time relaxing at a spa.

The ten days spent at the spa were wonderful. When it was time to go back to New York, Steve looked at Leslie and remarked, "This is the first vacation I've had in my career, where I don't have to go back to work. Why don't we extend a few days and drive up to Sedona?" At that point, Leslie had never heard of Sedona but was in no rush to go home, so a couple of extra vacation days in a spot Steve said was beautiful sounded good. Leslie says, "I had no idea what to expect." The next day they drove north.

They exited I-17 at the Sedona exit then drove north toward the VOC. "And then it happened. We went around a bend in the road and all I could think to say was, 'WOW.' There before us were these huge towering, protective gentle giants made of red rock surrounding us as far as the eye could see. I have seen many large cities around the world with huge man-made structures of steel, glass and concrete, but nothing like this – and this was created by nature. I suddenly felt a sense of peace and safety and knew we needed to live here," says Leslie. Leslie was surprised at her reaction to the small town tucked away amid these towering red rock giants because, as she says, "I'm a big city girl. Always have been. I love the hustle, variety, fabulous restaurants and, of course, the shopping that is available in large cities."

They immediately began to investigate purchasing property in Sedona, but made no offers at that time. In early 2004, they returned to Sedona and began house hunting in earnest. They made an offer on a town-home at The Ridge in the VOC,[55] but inspection issues caused the deal to fall apart.

---

55 The Ridge is a Town-home community in the Village of Oak Creek

"We flew out again in May 2004 and found our home. We spent two winters in Sedona and summers on the Jersey Shore before deciding to move to Sedona full-time," says Steve.

What Steve and Leslie were looking for in a retirement home was very different. Steve hates high humidity and the cold, but loves the heat. Leslie likes warm weather but wanted some humidity. And the location relative to their children was a consideration. With children located in Arizona, California, Illinois and New Hampshire, they knew they would have to do some traveling or have the children travel to Sedona for the family times during the holidays that is so important to them. The pull to live in Red Rock Country, even with those considerations, could not deter Steve and Leslie from deciding to move to Sedona.

"We love the fact we can hear birds singing when you step outside and the majestic beauty of Sedona, with blue skies, great sunsets and stars at night. We love the mild four-season climate and small town feel with large city amenities. The people are friendly because everyone is from somewhere else so they know what it is to be 'new' here. Everyone who lives here does so because they chose to – not because they have to. We made more friends here in the first year than anywhere we have lived. Sedona is destined to remain a special place with special value. To anyone thinking about moving here – don't wait. There will never be a better time to buy a home in Sedona."

Mark and Ann's Story

In 1999, Mark attended a professional meeting hosted by Arizona State University, but held in Sedona. He and his wife, Ann, flew into Phoenix's Sky Harbor Airport on an October evening, rented a car and drove north to Sedona on a beautiful but moonless night. The sky was so dark that they drove into the Sedona area without any idea of what they were missing; registered at their motel in West Sedona; ate a quick and late dinner at a nearby diner; then called it a night.

At sunup the next morning, they walked out onto the deck of the motel and their jaws dropped as they got their first look at Sedona's amazing red rocks. Within fifteen or twenty minutes, they were both saying, "I could live here." The professional meetings lasted for three days, and they spent almost every free minute exploring the town and Oak Creek Canyon.

They were both several years away from retirement at that point, but whenever vacation times could be coordinated, they returned to Sedona to check out real estate listings. They knew that they loved Sedona, but they both were cautious about financial matters and wanted to be absolutely sure that Sedona was the best choice. They agreed that Sedona's relatively high elevation (4,500 feet), with its resulting mild summer weather, was part of its attractiveness. They found a web site that listed towns in Arizona and New Mexico by elevation, and spent one of their vacations touring the Southwest, visiting towns with elevations at or above Sedona's 4,500 feet. There were several very interesting options, which included Flagstaff, Prescott, Strawberry/Pinetop, Payson, Show Low, Eagar, Bisbee in Arizona, and Silver City in New Mexico. But they decided that none of the alternatives came close to matching Sedona.

They bought a home in Sedona in 2001, and moved into it full-time when they retired in 2003. They didn't know anyone when they arrived, but quickly found that it's a very friendly town. Within weeks they had joined a hiking group and were meeting more and more Sedonans who had gone through a similar "Red Rock Fever" experience. Most Sedona transplants agree that it's difficult *not* to meet people and form friendships. For one thing, the weather is almost always sunny and mild, so neighbors are often outside. It's also true that Sedona is a tourist mecca, of course, and its residents tend to be active and involved, so new arrivals have plenty of opportunities to get involved as volunteers with organizations such as the Sedona Public Library, the Chamber of

Commerce Visitors Center, Red Rock State Park, Keep Sedona Beautiful, the Sedona Heritage Museum — too many to list here. Mark and Ann found that it's extremely easy to get to know people in Sedona, at least partly because most Sedonans share the experience of being drawn so strongly to the area that they were willing to make a major life shift to get here.

Mark and Ann say, "One word of caution: if you relocate to Sedona, be prepared (especially during the first year or two) to have plenty of house guests. But that's a small price to pay if you want to live in paradise."

Sedona Art Center located in Uptown Sedona

Traci's Story

Traci lived in Florida and was working in a high-stress marketing and website design position for a flight school. In 2009, her daughter wanted very much to see the Grand Canyon on her birthday so they planned a one week vacation to Arizona. Neither had been to Arizona before so they didn't know what to expect. They arrived at the Phoenix airport and drove north to Rimrock where some close friends lived. Rimrock is a small community located about 20 miles south of Sedona.

After visiting the Grand Canyon, they drove south to Sedona on their way back to Rimrock. It was then that Traci fell in love with Sedona. "I wasn't much in awe of the Grand Canyon, but I was totally in awe of Sedona. It was like I was drawn here," says Traci. She, her daughter and their friends went hiking, sightseeing and exploring in Sedona for the next few days. All too soon it was time to return to Florida. But Traci and her daughter were hooked on Sedona.

When they returned to Florida, Traci gave notice at her company; packed their belongings and left for Sedona. She didn't have a job lined up, but could stay with her friends while she looked for work.

Traci says, "It was very tough at first. The salaries offered for jobs in Sedona were much less than I was making in Florida. I held down two jobs at first. During the day, I worked as a reservation agent at a hotel and in the evening, I worked as a waitress, which I had never done before. But those jobs taught me a lot about Sedona."

Traci enrolled her daughter in a Charter School, which was about 20 miles from where they lived. Because there was no school bus, this proved to be financially costly since Traci had to drive her to and from school.

Traci is now the volunteer coordinator at a Sedona non-profit organization. She loves her work and is paid enough so that she doesn't have to work two jobs any longer. Traci says, "I love the energy of Sedona. The people are outgoing and friendly. As a single mom, I feel completely safe here. The past three years have been wonderful. I've met so many interesting people, from all over the world. Sedona is a very special place and I'm so thankful that my daughter and I can live here."

She likes the fact that there are no "big box" stores in Sedona but you can find them after a short drive. As far as advice to single people considering a move to Sedona, "It helps a great deal if you develop a support group, like a church or, if you have children, Big Brothers and Big Sisters."

Snoopy Rock viewed From Uptown Sedona

Jody's Story

Jody hasn't yet moved to Sedona but she is planning to do so someday. She discovered Sedona in 2001 while on a trip to the Grand Canyon. Her aunt had suggested that while she was in northern Arizona, if she had the opportunity to visit Sedona, she should do so.

As she entered Sedona from State Route 89A, she was struck by Sedona's beauty. Jody says, "What an awe inspiring backdrop to live and to visit. It was on that visit that I knew this was where I wanted to retire one day. The multicolored summits and bluffs radiating reds, oranges, yellows, burgundy and tan are nothing less than spectacular."

Jody, a professional photographer, is a few years away from retiring. She currently is working and saving her money in Orlando, Florida so that someday she can achieve her dream of living in Sedona.

"I envy the lucky residents who wake up to the beautiful scenery every day. When I retire, the biggest challenge for me will be to find the perfect house with the best view for the price. I love the majestic views and small town feel of Sedona. I hope that they limit development so that it will have that small town feel when I'm able to move there."

Jody advises those considering a move to Sedona, "Spend at least a week or two there on vacation to determine if it 'calls' to you."

Darryl and Lorna's Story

Darryl's first impression of Sedona was during a vacation trip from Massachusetts to Los Angeles in 1972. Driving down SR 89A in Oak Creek Canyon from Flagstaff through Sedona, "I was seeing beautiful views all the way."

In the early 1980s Darryl and Lorna were invited to spend a few days in Sedona with friends. Lorna says, "As we entered the Sedona area we were awestruck at the sight of a beautiful panorama of red mountains and the spectacular shape of Bell Rock. During the next several years we continued to visit Sedona. Although it was some years before either of us could retire, we decided to explore Sedona further as a potential area for retirement. We decided to honeymoon in Arizona visiting the Grand Canyon, Flagstaff and Sedona. While in Sedona, we contacted a realtor and had him show us buildable vacant lots."

After viewing many properties in the Sedona area, they decided that the quiet, small town, mostly residential, Village of Oak Creek was most desirable. They bought a lot that bordered the National Forest. The rest is history!

Darryl says, "During the next seven years we continued to familiarize ourselves with the area during different times of the year. We took a jeep tour; rented a jeep; went hiking; picnicked on Oak Creek; attended live theater at the local playhouse and just explored the Verde Valley. We knew that we could always sell the lot if we changed our minds. However, the more we visited, the more we realized that the next chapter in our lives should be in Sedona."

When Darryl retired, he decided to design their home. As a mechanical engineer who designed communication satellites as a career, designing a home seemed to be a natural for him. He was meticulous in attending to details, lot calculations, sun angles, etc. and creating their dream home was fun for him.

The December before Lorna retired, Darryl had selected a contractor to build their house. They rented a small condo close to the lot so Darryl could be on the site every day with the contractor. Three months later, Lorna retired and was on a plane to Arizona the following day. The home was finished in June that year. They returned to California to sell their condo which they were fortunate to sell in three days. The moving van was scheduled and their furniture was on its way to their new home. With great excitement they gave up the condo and moved into their new home.

Lorna says, "The Village is a very quiet residential community with few commercial establishments. Businesses are in West Sedona and Uptown Sedona. They are the tourist draw. We don't mind driving the eight miles up picturesque SR 179 to purchase something that is not available in the Village. After living in the LA area for many years and dealing with traffic congestion there, Sedona driving was, and still is, a breeze."

It took little time for Darryl and Lorna to become acquainted with nice folks from different parts of the U.S. They both began volunteering at Red Rock State Park. Darryl worked in the maintenance shop and Lorna did trail maintenance. Lorna also volunteered at the Community Center delivering Meals-On-Wheels. Darryl joined the Oak Creek Country Club and is enjoying playing golf. They also belong to a hiking group as Sedona has many interesting places to hike and explore. "We have developed a wonderful group of friends with many of the same interests as ours," says Lorna.

"Moving to the Sedona area was a major environmental change from congested city life. We had no problem acclimating to a quieter life style. Many conveniences that we took for granted were no longer available without an hour or more drive. These are things to consider before moving to this area. Also the weather is a factor. We do have four seasons albeit the fall and spring are short. The winter temperatures get cold at night and usually in the 50s during the day. The summer gets into the 90s and low 100s. We may get a dusting of snow several times in the year and late winter and late summer rains. The skies are clear and deep blue often with beautiful white clouds and the sunrises and sunsets can be spectacular. Sedona is truly one of the most beautiful places on earth."

Charlie and Marilyn's Story

About fifteen years ago, Charlie and Marilyn were planning their annual summer vacation. Their son was about 8 years old at the time and they had usually driven to Disneyland in their motor home and spent the time in southern California. This time, Charlie suggested that they travel east then south through Arizona and visit the Grand Canyon on the way to Disneyland. Marilyn checked out Arizona and found this mystical place called Sedona along the way so they arranged to stay in Sedona for a few days.

Marilyn says, "Sedona was so beautiful. It became part of our vacation plans for the next five years until we bought a house and moved here. Sedona is an absolutely gorgeous place. The striking red rock buttes with the tough green pinon pines and cactus plants seemingly growing right out of the rocks framed by a nearly always bright blue sky sold us on the area from the beginning. The hot dry climate also felt really good after a life of living beneath the Pacific's wet and cold coastal marine layer."

Charlie says, "When we decided to buy a home in Sedona, we soon learned that after retirement our California dollars would buy nearly twice the square footage as it would along the coast. The homes and views are also beautiful. Hard to beat anywhere. Sedona is also a smaller town than the suburban California we came from, which we really like."

When they moved to Sedona, they enrolled their son in the Sedona public schools. "We found the public schools to be excellent. There was no need to enroll him in a private school," says Marilyn.

The things we like most about Sedona are that it has a small town feel to it. "It's quiet and slower paced than where we came from. Arizona is a young state and we like the basic values, conservative approach of the government. Sedona itself is great for beautiful hikes and red rock views. Part of the reason we bought the house we did was that a trail head into Red Rock Country is just down the street from our front door. The spiritual community in Sedona is very open with several wonderful groups and venues for expanding your spiritual awareness."

Charlie and Marilyn suggest, "If you're thinking of moving to Sedona, check the property values carefully as they can vary greatly depending on location and the red rock views. Also be sure to have everything inspected as the desert heat can be hard on houses. Sedona is pretty much a vacation/retirement community. If you're not retired and not an artist or a services worker it will be hard to find work. This might mean a two hour each way commute to Phoenix each day for work. Some people do this and really look forward to the weekends."

Bell Rock

John and Roberta's Story

John and Roberta live in Ontario, Canada. They are the owners/operators of a bed and breakfast in the spring through fall months. For many years, they had escaped the Canadian winters by going to Las Vegas, not to gamble, but to hike in nearby Red Rock Canyon.

In 2006, they were sitting in a hot tub on the roof of the Venetian Hotel talking to another couple about Red Rock Canyon. The couple told John and Roberta, that, if they liked Red Rock Canyon, they would love Sedona. John and Roberta asked, "Where is that?" The next winter John and Roberta headed to Sedona for the first time.

"Before we left for Sedona, we searched out hiking clubs on the Internet and found the greatsedonahikes.com website. We made contact through the website and received lots of info about hiking and even about what to consider when renting a Sedona vacation home. We were invited to join the group for hikes on Mondays. We decided to join the hiking group. By doing so, we met all these wonderful friendly people who even invited us to join them for lunch - they know the best restaurants as well as the best hikes!"

As John and Roberta drove into the VOC on SR 179 they fell in love with Sedona. They got "Red Rock Fever" within minutes of first seeing the magnificent scenery. "We knew right away that we wanted to buy a second home in Sedona, but knew it could never be our permanent home as we are Canadians. We had a limited budget and, while condos were within our budget, they didn't suit our lifestyle. Single family homes were out of reach for us in 2007. So we carried on renting vacation homes every winter, but never found it totally satisfactory."

Then the housing crisis hit and like everywhere else in the U.S., Sedona home prices fell. "We were uncomfortable with the thought of benefiting from the misfortune of someone else, but as our realtor pointed out, things would get even worse if no one started purchasing homes."

They were very fortunate to find a modest 3 bedroom, 2 bathroom single family home for about half of what it sold for when new in 2006. They liked the home because it had a backyard which they felt could be turned into their very own private oasis. They have been amazed at how fast things grow in the desert and are pleased that their dream oasis is quickly becoming a reality.

John says, "We love being in Sedona. We love the scenery, the hiking, but most of all the people. We have made so many special friends and have an amazing social life in Sedona."

Roberta, a travel and real estate writer for the Toronto Star, advises new Sedona residents to, "Join a hiking club or a golf club, or a birding club. Whatever your interests, you'll find wonderful like-minded people."

Hikers enjoying the red rocks

Tom and Becky's Story

Tom and Becky became Sedona retirees in much the same way that many others came to the *Land of the Red Rocks*. They bought a timeshare. That was in 1999 and they actually spent their first vacation in Sedona back in 2000. The facility was brand new, and they hadn't been to Sedona since 1979, the year that they drove through Oak Creek Canyon on the way back from a conference at the Grand Canyon. The 1979 trip had left many indelible memories about the mysterious allure of the Sedona-Oak Creek Canyon scenery.

After at least three subsequent timeshare vacation trips to the Sedona area, it was clear that the town of Sedona offered more than scenic wonders, mild winters and great hikes. Tom and Becky had met a lot of new people and made several friends. Along the way they started exploring Sedona's neighborhoods and stumbled upon an open house in December 2003. That introduced them to a "buyer's agent" which started them checking their wherewithal and estimating when they could actually retire from both their jobs back East. One thing led to another and before they knew it, they had become serious buyers looking for a retirement home! After their first offer on a home had been turned down, they eventually succeeded in buying another existing home in a gated community in February 2004.

For the first four years, they gradually furnished and customized the house, in preparation for their final move. They made tentative plans to retire in 2008, and started thinking about how best to close out their individual Federal careers with the U.S. Army and the National Park Service.

Looking back on their decision, Tom and Becky know that they have chosen Sedona for at least three good reasons. First, they were long-time visitors to Southwestern parks. Tom's career as a historical architect with Delaware Water Gap National Recreation Area, a unit of the National Park Service (NPS), had a big influence in their quest to find an area that combined their love of park attributes, Western history and ancient cultures, all of which could be experienced in multiple ways in the Sedona landscape.

The second reason was an equally big influence on Becky's decision to move to Sedona. She discovered *Arizona Highways* magazine when she was a patient of one of her Philadelphia doctors who had traveled to Southwestern destinations. It was his collection of back issues that caught Becky's attention. She always looked forward to reading them! "I could really imagine myself living in this sun-swept state! I was young then, and hadn't completed my educational objectives or fulfilled my career goals. And yet, there it was .... the never-ending labyrinth of Arizona highways that seemed to beckon me into a world of new possibilities," says Becky.

The third reason for their move to Sedona was the insatiable need for adventure. Tom and Becky had always had interests in natural history and archeology, along with art and photography. It wasn't just the call of the canyons or the allure of outdoor living that made Sedona and the Verde Valley so appealing. It was the opportunity to participate in mineral prospecting activities. Rockhounds in local clubs with a passion for fossil collecting and gem cutting made club membership for Becky an exciting opportunity. She'd had a lifelong enthusiasm for geology and paleontology, and here was the ultimate frontier! Arizona was a state with an endless array of mineral deposits and mining operations. It was also a vortex center and a UFO hot spot! "Now I had fellow boomer retirees who shared my interests in field collecting and Ufology. The new adventures proved irresistible. These new attractions led me to become a certified UFO field investigator with the Mutual UFO Network (MUFON). And Tom became a member of a free spirited men's club, a discussion group where a wide array of professional backgrounds and interests converged."

"Without hesitation, we both feel Sedona offers the perfect home base for retirees who have an interest in the arts and sciences. What more could one ask for in the way of opportunities and services, plus rockhounding and all the rest? We rest our case!"

Tom and Peg's Story

It has been said of Montana that it is one of the last best places. Tom and Peg couldn't agree more. They have loved living in Montana for the last 25 years, but decided they needed a place to escape the state's long, cold winter months.

In their early 60s, Peg and Tom have tried all kinds of outdoor activities. They especially like fly fishing and hiking. When they decided to spend the winters in a warmer climate, a priority was easy access to hiking. They knew they would never duplicate the fishing in Montana, but since they were going to spend the summer in Big Sky country, maybe that would be enough.

Tom and Peg also enjoy the quality of life in a smaller town, where people are friendly and, even if you don't know everyone personally, you would at least become a familiar face at the grocery, coffee shop and hardware stores. Tom and Peg knew that, for them, developing new friends would be essential to their enjoyment of a community. They hoped to find new friends to hike with, share some food and wine and trade stories.

Sedona wasn't the first place Peg and Tom investigated. They spent time in some other Arizona locations, as well as some smaller communities in southern Utah. But, like the story of the three bears, the locations were either too big or too small, too urban, too rural, too cookie-cutter. Nothing was exactly what they were hoping for.

Tom and Peg's first experience in Sedona was a month-long stay in a house they rented in the Chapel area. As they drove up from Phoenix, they experienced the typical jaw-dropping reaction to their first views of the red rocks. "We actually get to stay here for a month? WOW!" Views of the red rocks were magnificent, and since their rental house had a hot tub, they quickly understood why the area's dark skies were so important for star gazing – which became a new interest for them, especially while soaking in the rental home's hot tub after a long hike.

During their first month-long visit to Sedona, Peg and Tom participated in an informal weekly hiking group. The group would meet every Monday morning and hike for a couple of hours, then head to one of the local restaurants for lunch.

Peg and Tom decided to buy a home in Sedona. They remember the day the decision was made vividly. It was a brilliant blue sky day in February, and they were out on one of their favorite Sedona hiking trails. The predicted high was to be 60 degrees and they were working up a little bit of a sweat in their light fleece jackets. Tom had looked at the Montana weather report before they left the house: the high that day was expected to reach a balmy 10 below zero! While they were on the trail they looked at each other and laughed about how lucky they were to be able to be out enjoying such great weather, not shivering in Montana's deep freeze!

Not only was the weather great, but they were enjoying their time in Sedona with several new friends. Sedona seems to be blessed with an abundance of very friendly and open people who love to get together over a glass of wine or casual dinner.

They realized that Sedona was, perhaps, another last best place.

With the decision made to purchase a Sedona residence, Tom and Peg began working with a local real estate agent. Since their plan was to be in Sedona for several months each year, they decided against a condo and focused on single-family homes.

It took several trips over the summer before they found a house. The real estate market was still recovering from the housing bubble. There were not a lot of houses on the market that met their criteria; and prices were lower but not bargain basement.

They looked in all areas of Sedona, and ultimately purchased a home in West Sedona. In retrospect, Peg and Tom think they should have given more consideration to the Village of Oak Creek. Their West Sedona location is convenient to trails and shopping, but the trade-off is busier streets and a more frenetic pace.

In addition to time outdoors, Tom and Peg enjoy activities with their Sedona friends and neighbors. Tom is a long time "rockhound" so they joined the Sedona Rock and Gem Club. They also joined and support the Verde Valley Archeology Center, participating in their meetings and going on numerous field trips. The Archeology Center, along with some hikes to "secret spots" with friends, sparked a new interest in Native American ruins and rock art which are found throughout Sedona and the surrounding National Forest.

The Sedona Public Library is another resource the couple enjoy. It offers free computer use and wifi access, especially handy when in transition from one home to another. It is also the location for many different club meetings. For newcomers, it is a way to learn about the surroundings. When the desert plants were blooming outside, the library had a display about plant life. Montana's plant life is quite different than Sedona's, and with the help of friends, Peg and Tom are learning how to recognize many Arizona plant types and wildflowers.

Of course, no place is perfect. Traffic can be a problem. There is not a direct connection between the Village and West Sedona, and this can make for fairly lengthy drive times. Special events and large influxes of tourists can tie up traffic. There aren't many shortcuts through neighborhoods, but that's actually a good thing for residents.

Montana doesn't have a sales tax, so Sedona's 10-plus percent sales tax seems high to Tom and Peg. They realize that the high sales tax is at least partly balanced against lower property taxes, but still it adds up, especially on big purchases.

The metaphysical experience is visible throughout Sedona. While it's not something they are into, they keep an open mind. "One of the things we love about Sedona is that the people are very tolerant of many points of view. It fosters a spirit of openness and kindness that is really special," says Peg.

After spending their first full winter in Sedona, the couple feels they have just scratched the surface of what is available. "Sedona attracts people who are still interested in learning, doing and growing – and that is just what we want as we enter our retirement years!"

86

Index

Cathedral Rock, Sedona's most photographed rock formation

Made in the USA
Lexington, KY
12 January 2014